The Way of Kabbalah

By the same author
TREE OF LIFE
ADAM AND THE KABBALISTIC TREE

Zev ben Shimon Halevi

The Way of Kabbalah

Rider & Company

London Melbourne Sydney Auckland Johannesburg

Rider and Company Ltd
An imprint of the Hutchinson Publishing Group
3 Fitzroy Square, London W I P 6JD
Hutchinson Group (Australia) Pty Ltd
30–32 Cremorne Street, Richmond South, Victoria 3121
PO Box 151, Broadway, New South Wales 2007

Hutchinson Group (NZ) Ltd
32–34 View Road, PO Box 40–086, Glenfield, Auckland 10

Hutchinson Group (SA) (Pty) Ltd
PO Box 337, Bergvlei 2012, South Africa

First published 1976
Reprinted 1980

Set in Monotype Bembo

Printed in Great Britain by The Anchor Press Ltd
and bound by Wm Brendon & Son Ltd
both of Tiptree, Essex

ISBN 0 09 125410 8 (hardback)
ISBN 0 09 125411 6 (paperback)

For
Yoshua ben Shimon Hakham Halevi
my grandfather and first link.

Preface

Everyone is searching for something. Some pursue security, others pleasure or power. Yet others look for dreams, or they know not what. There are, however, those who know what they seek but cannot find it in the natural world. For these searchers many clues have been laid by those who have gone before. The traces are everywhere, although only those with eyes to see or ears to hear perceive them. When the significance of these signs is seriously acted upon, Providence opens a door out of the natural into the supernatural to reveal a ladder from the transient to the Eternal. He who dares the ascent enters the Way of Kabbalah.

Spring 5734

Contents

Illustrations

Introduction

Every mystical tradition aims at union with the Ultimate One. This state of total realization is obtained by balance and the raising of consciousness up through all the levels of Existence to the source itself. Such a condition is rare, even though it is everyone's birthright, because few appreciate the laws that govern the universe and human development.

It is the task of a spiritual tradition to set out these laws and show how to apply them. While it is true that approaches may differ, according to period and custom, the law that opposites complement each other, for example, is quite recognizable in the relationship between practice and theory. In the mystical tradition of Israel these active and passive aspects of the Torah or Teaching are called practical and speculative Kabbalah. As studies they provide the necessary training for direct experience. Kabbalah means 'to receive', and this is only possible when the two disciplines are united in a man's being. Such a spiritual event expresses in human terms the law of the triad which brings the universe into existence and returns it to its origin again.

From the One to the appearance of opposites and their relationship is a step out of infinity into the finite world. Here is the beginning and end of relativity, with energy, form and consciousness in a diverging and converging complex stretched between All and Nothing. The objective laws that govern the universe are described by the chief diagram of Kabbalah known as the Tree of Life. This analogue model of the Absolute, the World and Man is the working key to speculative and practical Kabbalah. By living the Tree the Kabbalist experiences its reality, so enabling him to rise safely and secure a foundation in the upper levels of Existence. If he is truly established there he may be given perceptions and knowledge of matters unobtainable in this world, or be the channel by which the influx of Grace descends from above. If this be so, he fulfils his purpose as incarnate Adam, directly harmonizing with the Will of his Maker throughout all Earths, Edens and Heavens. In such a state he may even rise in the Chariot of his Soul to the Throne of the Spirit upon which sits the Eternal Adam, the Divine Man, the last separate realization before complete union with the Ultimate One.

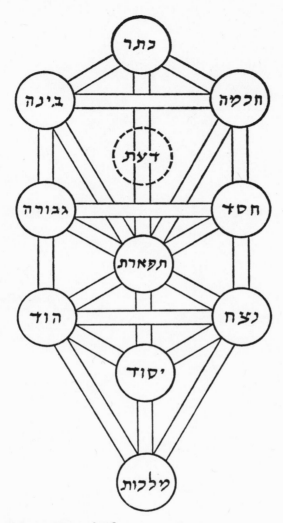

Figure 1. Sefirotic Tree of Life.

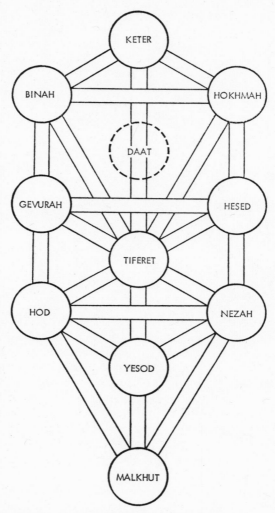

Figure 2. Hebrew Tree: English Transliteration.

1
The Tradition

In every religion there are always two aspects, the seen and the hidden. The manifest is observed in buildings, ministers, rituals and scriptures. These perform the task of influencing the world at large by bringing a sense of a higher Power, a Moral code and good customs into what for the mass of people is a tooth-and-claw existence. Of course there are times when the ministry becomes influenced by the ways of the world, and its authority is corrupted, turning it into the oppressor of the soul as well as the body. But such phenomena are subject to the laws of cosmic justice, and the evil destroys itself. Every religion has had such periods, and they indicate the last phase of decay before a new impulse enlivens the tradition again.

The new impulse always originates from the hidden aspect of the religion. Often centred on one man or a group, the light that once illuminated the Teaching returns to meet the needs of a generation that can no longer accept its parents' understanding of the tradition. This process must occur continuously in order to preserve the life of a religion. When it does not, the inner meaning soon fades into mere form, which then turns into dead custom that imprisons the ignorant and drives the intelligent away. The irony and providence of such a situation is that the rebels often seek and find the original principles of their faith far away from the conventional and conservative establishment of their own religion. Indeed, often while examining the source of another tradition they recognize the same precepts and objectives, and sometimes in terms strangely more familiar than the watered-down or silted-up versions they were instructed in as children. This is because at source all traditions meet.

This source is the hidden aspect of a tradition that periodically manifests when those responsible for the spiritual life of mankind reformulate the Teaching for the current generation. This restatement of the nature of Man and his relationship to the World and God takes many forms but it is never changed in essence. The Teaching is complete and perfect, although it wears many garments.

The hidden aspect of religion is to preserve the tradition, but not by rigid code. Thus, while the Teaching is written down, or designed into festival, art or story, its real life can only be imparted orally, that is in the subtle relationship between elder and younger. In this way there is no distortion as the language of the past becomes blurred with time. Each generation is taught in its own tongue, so that while terms may change the precise meaning in a current idiom does not. This is why many scriptures of long ago are unintelligible; we sense the profound truth of them but we cannot fully comprehend the language or symbols, because they were written for the children of that time. This does not mean that all writings are invalid. There are some like the Bible that are so simple and objective that the Teaching speaks across the millennia. The stories are basic, with no technical complexity. For example we can see in the journey of the Children of Israel out of Egypt and to the Promised Land the travail of the soul leaving the bondage of the body and its difficulties before entering the land flowing with milk and honey. Such scriptures are of quite a different order to the many learned works and textbooks of religion. Every religion has its scriptures, and they are the grounding of that tradition in relation to the World at large. None of the major faiths could exist without them.

The inner Tradition is a continuous line. Kabbalah, it is said, goes back to the angels who were instructed by God. Mankind is taught by the chief Archangel Metatron, who Apocalyptic Legend says is the transfigured Enoch, the man who walked with God and did not taste death (Genesis 5:24). Metatron, legend says, has manifested throughout history as various great teachers, one of whom may have been Melchizedek, the king without father or mother, who initiated Abraham into the line (Genesis 14:18-20). Abraham in turn taught his son Isaac, who passed the Teaching on to Jacob. When Jacob became Israel, the father of the twelve types of all humanity, only Levi was capable of transmitting the Teaching. Moses, a Levite, continued the line, passing it on to Joshua and the Elders of Israel. David, the first real king of Israel, had a direct connection with the Tradition, as his blessing of Solomon indicates in his use of the attributes of God (I Chronicles 29:11). Solomon possessed the key but lost it when he drifted off into the worship of other gods. This caused the ending of the kingdom and the eventual destruction of the Temple, which symbolized and embodied the Teaching in its architecture. With the outer manifestation gone, the Teaching went underground during the Exile to Babylon, but returned again with the Great Assembly of Ezra. From here on it ran parallel to orthodox Judaism, but always discreetly hidden, so that while the learned studied the Bible and its commentary, which became the Talmud, there were also those who contemplated and practised the Maaseh Berashit – the Work of Creation, or study of the Universe – and the Maaseh Merkabah – the Work of the Chariot, or the study of Man. Both these studies were considered highly secret; and yet, as with all esoteric doctrines, they remained concealed not because anyone hid them but because they were simply unintelligible to anyone who had no interest in the upper worlds. Like all such studies much misunderstanding grew round them, sometimes because those who thought they knew, imagined they had an exclusive right to the knowledge and frightened inquirers away as intruders, or because of sheer superstitious ignorance, especially by those who understood only a little of the implication of spiritual work. This phenomenon has dogged mystics in every religion. St John of the Cross was hard pressed by the Church, and not a few Sufis were persecuted by orthodox Islam. Mystics within Judaism had the same problem, and some, like the Essenes, formed isolated communities to protect themselves.

The Kabbalah, although it was not called this until the Middle Ages, was present both in Palestine and the Babylonian community throughout the Roman period. By this time it had absorbed many Greek and Babylonian words and ideas, adapting them to the Jewish mystical Tradition in order to speak to the generations who lived within the cultures of these Empires. Such books as the Sefer Yezirah illustrate the blend well; and other works, like the Book of Enoch, indicate that prophetic revelation was far from dead despite the powerful Gentile flavour of the text.

The line continued through the early Christian era, and there is no doubt that Joshua ben Miriam, or Jesus, was well acquainted with the hidden Jewish Tradition. His whole outlook and frame of reference is Kabbalistic: thus, for example his term 'Kingdom of Heaven' directly refers to the Malkhut of Beriah. On the orthodox front the Work of the Chariot was continued, the Talmud calling its practitioners the Merkabah travellers or 'the Frequenters of Paradise'. This period created a literature based on their experiences. Such spiritual excursions to the various stages of ascension were described in terms of Heavenly Halls, the Throne of God, and, in one work, a description of the Divine Adam and his dimensions. These books were regarded by those in charge of the mainstream of Judaism as too potent for ordinary folk to handle. Indeed, many rabbis forbade their study and insisted on concentrating only on the reasoned logic of the literal Torah which dealt principally with righteous conduct in this world.

The Hokhmah Nistarah, the Hidden Wisdom, remained concealed by its very nature and continued on as the discreet practice of a few over many centuries, until it was transmitted to Italy by Aaron ben Samuel from Babylon in the middle of the ninth century. From here it spread north into Germany, to give rise to a very practically orientated Kabbalah, and west to France and Spain, to generate the more speculative branch. This philosophical trend in the Western Mediterranean was stimulated by the revival of Greek learning in Moslem Spain. To counteract the attraction of Aristotle, Kabbalists reformulated the Teaching into the acceptable academic language of the time. As Kabbalah already contained many Neoplatonic terms, the adaptation was successful; indeed so much so that there was a major flowering of Kabbalism parallel to the great movement of scholasticism in Christendom. The geographical focus of Kabbalistic study lay in Provence and Spain, particularly the Catalan town of Gerona, where much important speculative work was done on Kabbalistic theory.

Out of this great surfacing of the Tradition came what is generally recognized as Kabbalah. It was crystallized in the massive literary work known as the Zohar or Book of Splendour which contains a vast amount of esoteric material dating back to Roman times. As such, despite the fact that it was considered at best a compilation and at worst a brilliant forgery by its author Moses de Leon, it became the authoritative canon for written Kabbalah. Orally the Teaching remained discreet, although each generation spoke of it and wrote it down in terms that it could understand. Isaac Luria, a Kabbalist who lived in sixteenth-century Palestine, was the last major re-interpreter of the Tradition. While none of his writing survives, his influence in the speculative field and in practice are still with us today, although in fragmented form. The line still continues after passing through many events in Jewish history, some of them as catastrophic to the Tradition as to the people involved in them. The seventeenth-century false messiah Sabbatai Zevi shook the image of Kabbalah into discredit for several centuries; and the borrowing of its terms and diagrams by aspiring magicians for very un-Kabbalistic purposes brought its name into much disrepute. The magical use of Kabbalah had already happened amongst Jews during bad periods of persecution; but this occurs in all peoples when under extreme duress. The line in its pure form did however proceed despite these difficulties and manifested among the Hasidim of eastern Europe and the Oriental Jews, who had picked it up from the Sephardi or Spanish and Portuguese exiles of the fifteenth century, who had spread out over Europe, north Africa and the Turkish Empire.

All formulations of a tradition are initiated, grow, fulfil their purpose, decay and die. Often, however, many who are on the periphery of such a movement do not recognize that the light has been removed, that the heart has gone from the formulation and that all that is left is a set of redundant rules. The unperceptive often mimic the master, even don his role, and teach without depth and without realization of the precepts. They perform by rote because they have never experienced the Teaching. Nor can they, without a major change in their being. History reveals many such spiritual bodies that have died and become the precise reverse of what their founders conceived them to be. Schools originally designed to help people to free themselves spiritually can become psychological prisons. Such a training situation is dangerous for the seeker in pursuit of truth or mystical experience. To have as a master a man who is simply aping his own teacher or, worse, living out a long-dead myth is useless. In such a case help can come to a genuine aspirant, but not through the authority of a formal dynasty. Contact with the hidden tradition can be direct and unmistakable. This is the untraceable line of connection that scholars never find. It is the truly oral tradition. The result may be spectacular, like Ezekiel's vision by the river Cheber, but it is more likely to be an apparently well-arranged happening, a psychological change of attitude or an encounter that will alter the course of a whole life. All that is required for such an event is a total commitment to spiritual growth.

With this prerequisite, Grace and Providence can set up the conditions for an inner and outer change. Such turning-points are very rare; but then people who are prepared to risk all for a pearl of great price are not common. In time, and always just at the right moment, a teacher or maggid arrives. He may manifest in many ways, as old Kabbalistic documents indicate. One may not see him more than once, or realize one has known him all his life. It can be one's grandfather or a fellow-student, the man crossing the sea with you on a boat, or someone you thought a fool. He may arrive at your front door or already be in the house. No one can know who your maggid is except you and he. Kabbalah can only be imparted face to face. It is an oral tradition, which, while being given and received in the idiom of today, is a continuous conversation that has been carried on over many centuries.

The purpose of this book is to show the steps up Jacob's ladder. It sets out the theory and practice of the Tradition in ancient and modern terms, so that a sense of what Kabbalah is about may be grasped – for no book can ever convey the reality of the Tradition unless it is present already in the reader. For my part I continue the work my fathers gave me. I write in order to pay my debt, impart what I know; because, as one Kabbalistic maxim states, 'One cannot receive unless one bestows'. In this way the line continues until even our familiar world becomes quaint, old, then ancient to future generations. Then there will be, no doubt, others who will pick up the Tradition, be it by instruction or illumination. Perhaps you are the person; someone who reads these words in a faded book by a long-dead Kabbalist whose archaic phrases make some sense in a modern world far into my future. In Kabbalah time does not matter: only Eternity and beyond is our concern.

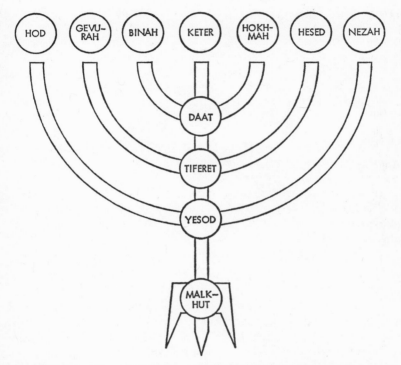

Figure 3. Menorah. *This design specified to Moses in Exodus is an earlier version of the Tree of Life. It has the active and passive sefirot to the left and right, with the central axis of equilibrium running down the central column. There were ten of these candlesticks in the Temple, one complete Tree within each sefirah of the Great Tree formed by their number.*

2
Language

Over its long history Kabbalah has appeared in many forms. They may, however, all be divided into four categories of comprehension. These are the literal, the allegorical, the metaphysical and the mystical. The origins of the first three levels of perception are rooted in natural man's faculties of sense perception, feeling and thought. In the untrained, one of these aspects usually predominates, so that a primarily instinctive person will see the world through the senses, a feeling type through symbols and moods, and a thinker through ideas. Under ordinary circumstances the fourth mystical view is not perceived by any of the others, although it can occur in all in rare and extraordinary moments of consciousness that raise one above the natural condition.

The appreciation that there are four traditional ways to approach Kabbalah explains why so much Kabbalistic literature is incomprehensible. Apart from the fact that it may not be in a modern idiom, only those writings related to our particular type will make any sense. Thus one book may describe elaborate rituals, another a world inhabited by angels, demons and apocalyptic dramas, while a third will spend several pages explaining the effect of a shift of balance in the Sefirotic Tree which will disturb all Existence. Even in ordinary matters, the doer does not understand the dreamer or thinker, and they in return regard him and each other as puzzles. It depends which natural type one is. Of mystical literature little can be said, because as many mystics have reported it is an indescribable experience, totally meaningless to the ordinary mind. All accounts are no more than dim after-images, and these are usually written up in one or other of the three lower forms of communication.

The Bible is possibly the best example of the four approaches. It may be seen as a literal history, as an allegory, or as a system of abstract ideas; and it also contains the mystical element.

An example of the various ways of appreciation is well demonstrated in the Temple of Solomon. From the physical view the design and building of it is described in great detail. We read in II Chronicles 3–4 of the kinds of material and techniques used, the number of workers, native and foreign, and even of the political and economic situation that allowed such a sumptuous building to be constructed. There is also documentation of the plan and how the site was laid out in three rising courts with the Temple at the apex of the complex. As such, the Temple was a powerful focus of religious, political and social attention. Built in Jerusalem, on the place where King David had prepared an altar, it was the greatest unifying factor in a nation that had been plagued by tribal conflict. To the physical man the Temple was where the nation met, where the rituals of worship of the God of Israel were carried out. It was there to be seen, visited and used. While he might not understand what went on during the ceremonies, he did sometimes experience a moving presence that was unmistakable. If called on he would fight and die to preserve the Temple, and ultimately many did who saw it as the literal manifestation of their religion, nation and personal identity.

The allegorical approach reveals quite a different view. Besides being the religious heart of the nation, its symbolism expressed the commitment of a people dedicated to proclaim and obey the divine Laws cut into the tablets of stone resting in the Holy of Holies. The act of building the Temple was, moreover, not just for Israel. It was ordained to be an example to the surrounding heathen peoples. Should Israel meet its Covenant with God, all would prosper. Should the Covenant be broken, the destruction of the nation and the ruin of the Temple would become a symbolic byword for forsaking the ways of the Lord. This Covenant, sealed with Solomon and first broken by him, was to be played out in history. Indeed so emotive is the emblem of the Temple that its rebuilding, desecration and final destruction are still commemorated to this day by Jews all over the world. Moreover the allegory is so powerful and full of meaning that the Temple has also passed into Western mythology, its form and content being used by the Church, the Freemasons and even a fraternity of Knights, the Templars. According to one great Kabbalist, the body is the Temple, and the keeping of the Covenant still relevant to the promise made to Solomon.

Seen from an intellectual standpoint, the Temple again becomes something quite different. Metaphysically the three ascending levels of outer, inner and priest courts can be regarded as the three lower Worlds of Manifest Existence in relation to the fourth embodied in the Temple. The Temple is the place of the Divine Glory before whose porch stand the bronze pillars of Boaz and Jachin. These columns represent the active and passive poles of the World of Azilut. Within the Sanctuary are ten candelabra, each of which is based on the model used in the Tabernacle in the wilderness. The original Menorah, or seven-branched candlestick, expressed the Ten Principles or sefirot by which the world comes into existence. The three lights on the right define the active sefirot and the three on the left the passive. Where their branches join on the central stem and foot are the sefirot of equilibrium. These are crowned by the middle light of Holiness. Each of the ten Menoraot in the sanctuary represents one sefirah in the Great Tree of Azilut which they form together. Beyond lies the veil that hides the Holy of Holies wherein hovers the Shekhinah or Divine Presence. Thus the Temple site contains a complete metaphysical scheme.

Practically, the whole Bible may be seen in these three different ways. All speak of the Torah, that is the divine Laws of Existence and their application to Man. The rules are clearly set out and the rewards for good or evil conduct are well illustrated. For the Kabbalist the Bible has the fourth level of comprehension, that of the mystic. Indeed, it describes in great detail the nature of the upper Worlds and how to gain entry into them. However, the prerequisite is a state of being different from that commonly experienced by most people.

Everyone has had great moments of awakening. They are everyone's birthright. In them the world appears to be totally different and indescribable in ordinary terms. Such events may occur in incidents of shock or periods of calm, moments of love and hate or even in times of apparent indifference to life and death. Such clear, penetrating states often happen in childhood and form a profound impression, like memories of another country, which is indeed what they are. They do occur in youth and adulthood, but they fade and pass, as there is no way to sustain them. Drugs can precipitate them, but this is damaging to both the physical and psychological organism and is not to be recommended. To enter such a state at will and maintain it requires much training. This is the purpose of Kabbalah.

In earlier times those interested in the mystical aspect of the Bible studied two particular texts. These were the opening chapters of Genesis and Ezekiel. This was because the former described the unfolding of Creation as seen from above and the latter a vision of the universe as perceived from below. These studies, the Work of Creation and the Work of Chariot, were both theoretical and practical disciplines, and their objective was to raise the Kabbalist up from the natural into the supernatural worlds. However such excursions were not without hazard, because to enter another dimension safely one must have a firm foundation in this world as well as the next, which is why no one was allowed to study or practise Kabbalah until he was mature, if not in years, then at least in mundane terms. Stability is vital in Kabbalah. No one who seeks for the wrong reasons need apply, if only for his own sake. To play with the Truth is not encouraged, because the first stages of initiation are concerned with the image one has of oneself, and few can withstand the exposure of their illusions.

In the following account a synthesis of the first three methods of comprehension will be used to outline the theory and practice of Kabbalah. The mystical aspect the reader must find for himself by applying the principles described. He may then make contact with the Tradition either through the line of succession, or by direct revelation; that is, if it is willed from above. Meanwhile all that can be done is preparation.

We begin with a brief description of the Great Tree, remembering that all of the material is relative, because even Kabbalistic literature is in the language of the natural man and is no more than a kaleidoscope of a Unity that is incomprehensible to our undeveloped natural state. Only the Lord can work in absolutes.

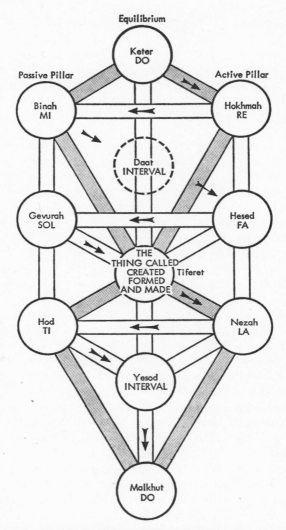

Figure 5. Lightning Flash, Octave and Two Faces. *Here the principle of progression is laid out as the impulse passes down from side to side of the Tree, with the crucial points crossed on the central column. The upper and lower faces illustrate the principle 'As above, so below', which applies throughout the Universe.*

3
The Great Tree of Azilut

God does not exist. God is beyond existence. God is Ayin – No Thing. Out of No Thing comes En Sof or the Infinite All. Within En Sof's boundlessness, Some Thing comes into unmanifest reality. It is hidden in the utter stillness and concealed within the complete silence. Some Kabbalists call this the Place without End.

Out of Endlessness comes the Will of En Sof. It retracts, or some say it concentrates, or even radiates, to allow the Manifest World to emerge out of the Unmanifest. The Will of En Sof coming out of concealment is called En Sof Aur, Light – *aur* in Hebrew – being the symbol of Will. The way in which the Light permeates Unmanifest Existence has been a matter of debate for many centuries. However, this is not a disagreement so much as a search for a way of expressing a Divine event, the full nature of which is only known to God. Many analogies have been put forward, but only as metaphors. Alas, they are often taken for the reality.

One analogy for the first manifestation of Will out of Unmanifest Existence is a dimensionless point. This dot of Manifest Existence is the source of everything that was, is and will be. It is I AM and in Kabbalah is called the First Crown, the Ancient One and the White Head. From here emanate the Ten Utterances that bring the relative World into being. In an instantaneous progression the Ten Divine Principles, the Attributes of God or sefirot, are realized like an eternal Lightning Flash. The sefirot are Keter or the Crown, Hokmah or Wisdom, Binah or Understanding, Hesed or Mercy, Gevurah or Judgement, Tiferet or Beauty, Nezah or Eternity, Hod or Reverberation, Yesod or Foundation, and Malkhut or the Kingdom. There is an eleventh non-sefirah between Binah and Hesed called Daat or Knowledge, but this performs a special role. There are several names to some sefirot, both in English and Hebrew. Gevurah, whose root is Might, is sometimes called Din or Pechad, which mean Judgement and Fear, and Hod and Nezah may be translated by Glory and Victory. The names used in this work are based on the original Hebrew root, so that Hod, for instance, when translated as Reverberation makes precise sense, while the word Glory tells us nothing of its sefirotic function, not to mention the fact that the term Glory is also used sometimes for Tiferet and the World of Azilut. Similarly, for Nezah we use the translation Eternity, which means in this sefirotic context to repeat or endlessly turn.

According to Tradition the word 'sefirot' means sapphires or sparkling lights. They have also been called Numbers, Degrees, Vessels, Powers, Garments, Crowns and many other names. This illustrates the flexibility of Hebrew and of Kabbalah. There is no hardened dogmatic form although the principles remain the same. In one century they were called the Inner Faces of God, in another the Primordial Days; this leads on to the subject of the arrangement of their progression.

Beginning with the One expressed in the First Crown, the perfect Manifest Unity divides into two, the second stage being an active manifestation. This was then completed by its passive opposite so that three sefirot came into existence out of the place of equilibrium. Moreover their relationship was not perfect, because the impulse of Divine Will had made a tension between them. Nevertheless in terms of a now relative existence they were in working balance, although this had constantly to be maintained. The three were, and still are, called the Supernals and represent the Eternal Divine within Manifest Existence. They are the Holy of Holies. Over the centuries the active and passive sefirot of the Supernal Triad acquired many analogical descriptions, but perhaps the most evocative are those of the Great Father and Mother. Their role in the complex system that was to follow was to head the two opposing and complementary poles or columns of Mercy and Severity, which in more earthly definitions are known as the pillars of Force and Form. It is said that Hokhmah or Wisdom was the

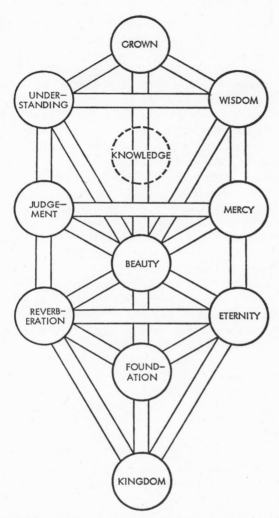

Figure 4. English Tree. *Translations of the sefirotic names vary. This is because a single Hebrew word can have several meanings. In this scheme Reverberation and Eternity are applied because they are the closest to the sefirotic functions of Hod and Nezah. All the names in fact only convey a fraction of the scope of each Sefirah.*

first thought after the impulse of Will emanating from Keter, the Crown and the Binah or Understanding was the passive formulation of the idea in the Divine Intellect. However, nothing further could happen until the Will from Keter, operating down the central column, helped the Lightning Flash across the gap occupied by the non-sefirah Daat to pick up the power of the active column again. This gap or interval is known as the Abyss, and is a crucial point in descending or ascending the Tree that is beginning to come into being.

The Impulse joins the pillar of Force at Hesed or Mercy, whose principle is that of expanding power. Here that which is manifesting grows and would dissipate itself if it were not checked by Gevurah, the principle of limitation. This illustrates how the sefirot work in pairs across the Tree, balancing and checking one another while being supervised from above and imparting power and control to those below. An unbalanced situation is described in early Kabbalistic literature which tells of the making of the first worlds. In them one or the other of the pillars predominated, so that one universe defused itself with overactivity and another collapsed into itself in excessive contraction. 'Without Severity or Judgement', says the Talmud, 'the World would have excessive evil, and without Mercy existence would be unbearably rigorous.' When sufficient equilibrium was obtained the universe became stable, but only within certain limits. Anything out of this relative norm becomes dangerous to it and generates what is symbolically known as evil. The economy of the body is a parallel. Any molecular, cellular or physical excess of growth or of restraint – of Force or of Form – causes it to be ill and sometimes die. As balance is critical in the human organism, so it is in the Great Tree upon whose principles the body is modelled.

Continuing the Lightning Flash, the relationship between Hesed and Gevurah helps to form in their synthesis the sefirah Tiferet or Beauty on the central column. This lower triad is called by some Kabbalists the triad of Divine Emotion and Morality. The title has no meaning at this point but it will later when we apply the Tree to Man, who is made in the same image as his Maker. The application of the word 'emotion' to the World of Azilut or Emanation caused much trouble for Kabbalists through the ages, because their more literal brethren always saw everything in natural terms. Several Kabbalistic works outlining the nature of the Divine World were disapproved of by the orthodox establishment of the period as making an image of God contrary to the Second Commandment. But this Commandment applies to the Absolute beyond even Existence. The Azilutic World, to which most of these documents referred, is already several removes from Ayin or No Thing, and the detailed descriptions written up in the visionary book, the Shiur Komah, and even Zohar were no more than outlines of Adam Kadmon, the Primal Man. The head, the beard, even the Divine body and its dimensions described were only metaphysical symbols to illustrate the nature of the World of Azilut. Without these analogues, natural man would have no information on the World of Emanations. This is why the Tree of Life became the most acceptable symbol in Kabbalah; not only did it contain all the information required for theory and practice, but it was an image of nothing literally seeable in the heavens above or in the earth beneath.

The sefirah Tiferet is the heart of the Tree. It lies halfway between the top and bottom sefirot on the column of equilibrium. As the central focus it performs a vital task, for it joins and reconciles the flow of various paths that come through its junction station. It is called Adornment as well as Beauty, because it is the result of the other sefirot, and unlike them has no particular function, other than to be. It is called the Seat of Solomon, for the obvious reason that it has access to Wisdom and Understanding, Mercy and Judgement, as well as the sefirot below it. Placed beneath the non-sefirah of Daat (Knowledge) it is also named 'Thou' or 'The Holy One, blessed be He'. These names refer to the manifestation of the Presence of God in the heart of Existence.

Tiferet forms with the two lower sefirot of Hod and Nezah the beginning of a reflection of the three Supernals but on a lesser level. The geometric figure composed of Keter, Hokhmah, Binah and Tiferet is repeated by Tiferet, Nezah, Hod and Malkhut, with Daat and Yesod in the same relative positions. Known as the Upper and Lower Faces, they perform as an upper complex of Mercy and a lower complex of Severity, so that heaven and earth, yet another analogy of this relationship, reflect the left and right pillars but in the vertical axis. The moral triad of Mercy, Judgement and Beauty forms a separate triangle between the two Faces that is crucial in the relationship between the upper and lower parts of the Tree, in the Divine as well as in Man.

Nezah or Eternity and Hod or Reverberation perform as the lowest working sefirot of the two outer functional pillars. Nezah on the column of force cycles power into the complex while Hod reverberates the impulse throughout the Tree. This is possible because, as will be remembered, there were ten menoraot in the Temple, that is one complete miniature Tree within each sefirah of the Great Tree of Azilut. This facilitates intersefirotic relationships and enables each sefirah to possess an active and passive aspect as well as all the qualities of the sub-tree that composes it. The idea of trees within Trees was developed by some Kabbalist into many levels of subtle underlay. (Each Kabbalist has his particular interest.) In the Divine Names attributed to the Tree that of Hosts is ascribed to Hod and Nezah, each carrying the active and passive aspect of the Divine, so that the various tasks to be carried out can be implemented. The image of Nezah and Hod as the right and left legs of the Primal Man, Adam Kadmon, indicates their function as supports.

Yesod, the Foundation of the Sefirotic Tree, performs as the last interval of an octave developing down from the first Do of Keter. In this musical analogy the notes Re and Mi are played by Hokhmah and Binah with the first interval at Daat. Hesed performs as Fa with So at Gevurah. Tiferet on the mid-point is the essence of the octave, its place containing all that has been brought into existence and all that will be manifest. It has no note of its own because it is all of them in the Great Monochord stretched between the end and the beginning and back again. Nezah and Hod take the impulse on down to the last interval before it hits the sefirah of Malkhut that absorbs in its composition of force, form and consciousness the densest but richest combination of Divine substance. The relationship between Yesod the Foundation, and Malkhut the Kingdom is very particular, because Malkhut is the only sefirah that has no direct connection with Tiferet. Yesod therefore is a bridge and a barrier to anything coming down or rising up, a very important point in the theory and practice of Kabbalah. Yesod sits at the centre of the lower face. As the focus of all the lower sefirot it performs as the first and last step in manifestation and realization, that is coming away from or returning to the Source of All, symbolized by Keter in the relative world. In Yesod the image comes into being and casts shape, life and will into the materiality of Malkhut.

Malkhut the Kingdom is said to be the dwelling place of the Shekhinah, the Divine Presence. Traditionally composed of the most elemental levels of the Divine World of Azilut, it represents the last stage in the calling forth, creating, forming and making of Adam Kadmon, whose feet touch the uppermost part of incarnated man. This sefirah situated at the bottom of the Great Tree is by no means the least important. Indeed, all the sefirot are equally important, because

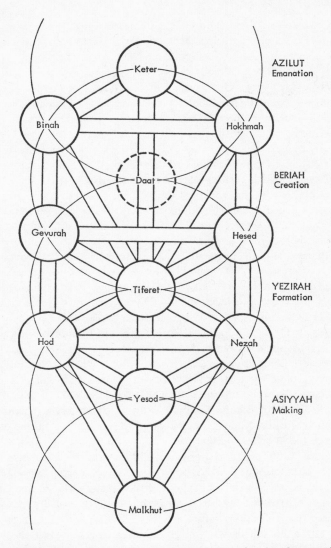

AZILUT
Emanation

BERIAH
Creation

YEZIRAH
Formation

ASIYYAH
Making

Keter

Binah

Hokhmah

Daat

Gevurah

Hesed

Tiferet

Hod

Nezah

Yesod

Malkhut

Figure 6. Four Worlds Within Azilut. *Contained within the Eternal World of Emanation are the four levels out of which the lower Worlds are generated. Although these levels are laid out in various ways by Kabbalists, all agree to the general principle that these four realms are present in this and all subsequent Trees.*

as the symbol of Adam Kadmon, the Primordial Man, illustrates, they are all part of a unified being. Malkhut is the last stage of Emanation, the Eternal realm above the World of Creation. Here the archetypal Tree of all the lower Worlds was completed and stabilized. Left was balanced with Right, above with below and all interconnected by a system of paths and triads that acted as a template for any complete organism that was to be subsequently created, formed and made. This arrangement contained all the laws required to run the Universe. It expressed in its Form, Force and Will the Oneness of All and its source. In this system was the complement of opposites, and the development of ten stages which related a series of triads to a central column of consciousness, which in turn was flanked by an active and passive set of triads attached to each functional side pillar. These triads, modelled on the supernal triangle, transmitted the Will descending from above to the furthest corner of the World.

As the octave of the Lightning Flash passes between the Crown and the Kingdom and back again, it also unfolds in four great stages expressed in the words of Isaiah 43:7: 'I have called, created, formed and made him'. These four levels inherent in the Azilutic Tree (see Fig. 6) generate three lower Worlds which periodically develop out of its unchanging Eternity into Time, that is Cosmic Existence with all its processes of birth, growth, decay and death. Such great universal cycles, called Shemittot, have fascinated some Kabbalists, and underlie the rarely understood word Jubilee which describes the end of a Cosmic cycle when all things return to the perfect state of the Divine Sefirotic World or Azilut. The brief of this study however is primarily concerned with the practice of Kabbalah, and so only an outline of the origin of the Worlds will be given.

Azilut is the World that was called forth out of the Unmanifest by the Ten Utterances of God. As Emanation emerges from En Sof Aur, so the separated Worlds emanate out of the four levels of Azilut. Thus, from the creative zone of the Divine comes the World of Beriah which manifests diagrammatically as a creative sub Tree springing from the midst of the Azilutic Tree. The impulse then continues, in that out of the cosmic World of Beriah emerges the Tree of the World of Formation, whose root lies in the Yeziratic level of Azilut. In the same way the Asiyyatic level of the World of Emanation generates the World of Making which comes out, in series, from the midst of Yezirah, thus completing a sequential scheme of three lower Worlds beneath, but contained in, a Divine World of Unchanging Unity.

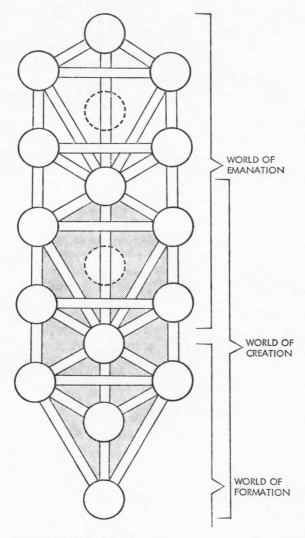

WORLD OF
EMANATION

WORLD OF
CREATION

WORLD OF
FORMATION

Figure 7. Emergence of Four Worlds. *Out of the World of Emanation emerges the World of Creation. From the lower face of Azilut comes the upper face of Beriah, which in turn creates in its lower face the upper face of Yezirah, and so on down to complete a ladder of four interfaced Worlds. This scheme is one of several that Kabbalists have used to describe the Universe.*

As there are several versions of how the four levels fit into the Azilutic Tree so there are various models of the four Worlds and their relationship to one another in Kabbalistic literature. These are all within a broad band correct and incorrect because they are all subjective views of an objective World. 'This is only from our viewpoint', said one early Kabbalist, and one must take into account where on the Tree he was looking from. Each level has quite a different outlook. For the purposes of this particular book one specific system has been adopted.*

*For a more detailed account of the Tree see the author's *Tree of Life*, Rider & Co., London, and Weiser, New York, 1972.

4
The Work of Creation

The World of Azilut is also known as the Divine Glory. Eternal and unchanging, it existed as a complete realm of Emanation before Creation began. In the total scheme of all the Worlds it is the place of interaction between the Will of En Sof and the changing Worlds beneath, where we live and have our incarnate being. In the Bible the opening verse describes the Creation of these lower Worlds with the words 'In the beginning God created the heaven and the earth.' The fact that in the original Hebrew the Name ELOHIM is used for God is most significant, because in Kabbalah this God Name signifies the severe or passive side of God, while YAHVEH represents the merciful and active aspect. These two are in Hokhmah and Binah relationship to EHYEH, the I AM of Keter. Together they make the Supernal triad which manifests below as the Creator or Keter of Beriah from where Creation begins. Moreover, by the use of the words 'In the beginning' we know that the process of creative manifestation has moved out of the Unchanging World of Azilut into the Time governed World of the Cosmos that is set out in the first chapter of Genesis.

The World of Creation emerges out of the Tiferet of Azilut, and not, as many students of Kabbalah are led to believe by a misunderstanding, out of Malkhut. This formula applies to quite a different operation.

The Tiferet of Azilut is the simultaneous Keter of Beriah, so that the lower face of Emanation is the upper face of the Tree of Creation. The principle is again repeated down through all the Worlds to our own, where we observe, for instance, that the psyche is interwoven with the body but not entirely subject to it. It also shows the connection and separateness of two distinct Worlds.

At the level of Emanation everything is purely Divine, at least from Keter to Tiferet, where Creation begins. Here in Tiferet is the fusion of all the upper Azilutic sefirot, or God Names. In Kabbalah the title of the lesser YAHVEH is used to define it. As the Keter of Beriah or Creation it contains the highest of created beings, Metatron, who acts as God's agent over all evolving creatures.

Out of this Crown of Creation emerge the other two Supernals of Beriah, its Hokhmah and Binah, which are simultaneously the Nezah and Hod of Azilut, the Hosts of YAHVEH and ELOHIM. They become the Father and Mother of the World below. The octave Lightning Flash then proceeds, and this is what is described in the first chapter of Genesis: 'And the Spirit of God [*Ruah ELOHIM*] moved upon the face of the waters.' The Abyss or Deep of the Beriatic Daat has been crossed, and the World of Yezirah, symbolized by water, has already been created, but as yet without form. The chapter goes on to tell how God called forth Light and divided the Day from the Night, that is he created the right and left pillars of the Tree of Beriah. The use of the word 'call' indicates we are still within the lower face of Azilut. The process is continued through several stages or days, until on the sixth day, that is the Asiyyatic level of Beriah, he makes a Man in 'our image, after our likeness'. This plural wording points out the operation of several aspects of the Creator. It also shows in the creation of Man, containing both male and female aspects, an androgynous Adam. This is the completion of the Beriatic Tree, at Malkhut, where all pillars converge again.

Many Kabbalists consider that the seven lowest sefirot on the Beriatic Tree are the seven Days of Creation. Others see the six outer sefirot as the Six Days between the first Do of Ketereiand the resolving Do of the Sabbath; the first and last being one. Another school sees the seven levels on the central axis of the Tree as the Days, with Man developing out of the Beriatic Yesod on the sixth Day as the image of God. All these views are valid according to which way one uses the law of octave and triad.

After the Lord (that is ADONAI, the God Name corresponding to

Malkhut) had rested in equilibrium on the seventh Day of Malkhut, He observed there was no man to till the ground. This means that while the upper face of Yezirah was inherent in the lower face of Beriah, there was nothing below to form the upper face of Asiyyah, symbolized in the word adamah or 'ground'. God therefore 'formed man of the dust of the ground': that is, God continued the Yeziratic Tree down to 'make' the world of elements and action, 'and breathed into his nostrils [*neshamet hyim*] the breath of life'. Here is Man in Eden, the Garden of that Yeziratic World which extends up into the Heaven of Beriah and down into the Earth of Asiyyah. Below, the lower face of Asiyyah became that part of Earth which lay beyond the gate of Eden. When Adam and Eve fell and were made to leave Eden, they descended into this lower Asiyyatic face to don animal skins, which we incarnate humans wear to this day in the form of the physical body. However, we still have in the upper face of Asiyyah a direct connection with the lower garden of Eden, and sometimes in certain clear moments we enter it, if only to glimpse its strangely familiar beauty.

Below and to the left and right of the three lower Worlds there is a realm known as the Kellippot (Qlipoth), or the Worlds of Shells. These are the phenomena created by forces and forms that are out of balance, that no longer have a conscious control or a constructive function in the Universe. Kabbalists give them the symbolic identity of demons and archdemons, which correspond negatively to the level of the angels in Yezirah and the archangels in Beriah. There are also elemental entities, which reside below, in and beyond the lower face of Asiyyah. All these phenomena for obvious reasons are not very helpful for development, which is why Kabbalists treat these worlds and their inhabitants with great circumspection.

We have now a very brief outline of the Great Tree of Azilut and the lower Worlds that emanate from it. As a totality it is the manifest relative universe, with many levels and a precise set of laws to govern it. The main laws may be summarized as follows: one, the Unity; two, the complementary opposites; three, the Great Trinity or Three Heads; four, the Worlds; five, the number of faces between the Keter of Azilut and the Malkhut of Asiyyah, sometimes called the Five Gardens; six and seven, the number of the side or lowest sefirot of Construction; eight, the notes of the Great Octave; ten, all the sefirot; and twenty-two, the number of paths connecting the Tree into a unity.

As has been observed, there are many ways of describing the same thing in Kabbalah, and versions of the extended Tree of the Four Worlds abound. Perhaps the first and most obvious is the symbol of Jacob's Ladder, which rested on the Earth where he slept and reached up to Heaven with 'the angels of God ascending and descending on it' (Genesis 28:12). Perceived in the form of a dream, God informs Jacob that He is always with him and that He will bring Jacob into the land whereon he lies. The symbolism of the dream indicates a quite different state of consciousness from Jacob's natural condition; indeed when he awoke he said: 'Surely the Lord is in this place; and I knew it not.' Full of awe, he then took the stone he had used as a pillow and set it up as an altar. After consecrating it with oil, the symbol of Grace from above, he called the place Bet El, the House of God. This stone has a traditional connection with a stone which the Holy One, Blessed be He, says the Zohar, cast into the Abyss during the Creation of the Worlds. The upper part of the stone, however, remained linked with its source, while its lower part descended to Left, Right and throughout Creation. Its name Shetiyah can be translated as Foundation; thus it relates the sefirah of Daat, the Abyss, with Yesod, the other Foundation. This connection can clearly be seen in the diagram of the interleaved Tree, where Daat and Yesod occupy the same sefirotic location, but in different Worlds. Both are crucial points, in descent or ascent of the Worlds. Tradition has it that this same stone was not only Jacob's pillow but the tablet upon which the Ten Commandments were to be cut. It was also, according to Biblical legend, the Foundation of Zion the Holy Mountain and the base of the sanctuary of David's and Solomon's Temple.

The vision of Ezekiel is the other major Biblical version of the four Worlds that is used by the Kabbalist. In this the prophet, like Jacob, underwent a change in consciousness that lifted him out of the state of natural bondage into a Yeziratic view of the levels above Asiyyah (Ezekiel 1). When the heavens were opened Ezekiel saw a vision of a wondrous chariot moved by four strange living creatures. Above the chariot, beyond a firmament, was 'the likeness of a throne', and upon the likeness of the throne was 'the likeness as the appearance of a man', who was 'the appearance and likeness of the Glory of the Lord'. Observe the repeated emphasis on 'likeness' and 'appearance', indicating a code of strict allegory. Here in symbolic form are again the Four Worlds. Ezekiel below by the river Cheber is in captivity in Babylon or Asiyyah. The Chariot and the Holy Living Creatures are Yezirah, with the Throne, beyond the veil of a firmament between the Worlds,

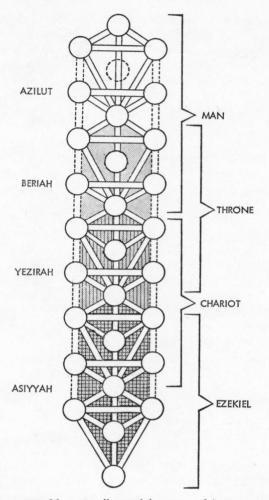

AZILUT

BERIAH

YEZIRAH

ASIYYAH

MAN

THRONE

CHARIOT

EZEKIEL

Figure 8. Four Worlds. *An allegorical description of the Four Worlds is found in the first chapter of Ezekiel. Here the upper Worlds are perceived from the point of view of incarnate man looking up from the level of a captive in Mundane Asiyyah. The likeness of a man seated on a throne carried in a chariot is Adam Kadmon. This is the Earth, Paradise, Heaven and the Divine Glory of God.*

representing Beriah. The man seated upon the Throne is Adam Kadmon, 'the Glory of the Lord' of Azilut. The fine detail that occurs throughout the account has given the Kabbalists much to study, for this is a carefully observed glimpse, but from below, of the Four Worlds described in the opening of Genesis.

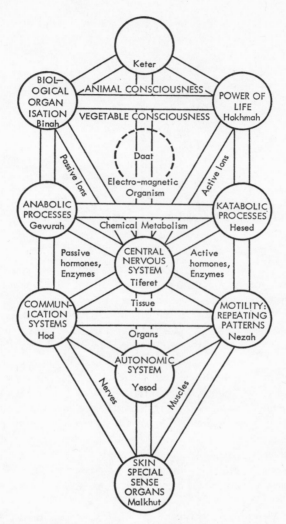

Figure 9. Physical Body of Man. *The biological organism is based on universal law. Therefore it can be expressed in terms of the Sefirotic Tree, the Kabbalistic model of all complete things great or small. Here the various levels of operation are set out in triads and sefirot to illustrate the microcosm of the body.*

5
Natural Adam: The Body

Before we can begin to ascend Jacob's Ladder we must become acquainted with our situation as Natural Adam. This is accomplished by examining the world about us in the light of Kabbalistic principles.

Man incarnate, that is, all those living on the earth today, exist at least in two of the Four Worlds. Based on the Asiyyatic Tree, natural man's being participates in pure organic form in the lower face of Asiyyah and in the bio-psychological process in the upper face of Asiyyah, which is simultaneously the lower face of Yezirah. In this way he has access to both Worlds. In traditional Kabbalistic terms, the lower face of Asiyyah is the lower Earth and the upper, the upper Earth, which is again simultaneously the lower face of Eden. Thus a natural man who at least is conscious of the upper or inner nature of his natural being has a contact with Paradise. For most people it is a dim memory of something long ago or far away, which they cannot recollect clearly, except in those rare moments of awakening out of the mundane or lower face of Asiyyah.

At the Malkhut of Asiyyah, in the lowest and densest state of materiality and consciousness in the Four Worlds, reside the four states of physical earth, water, air and fire, which go to compose and run the fleshly body. As such, the four elements interact in an ever-changing round of Force and Form which we know as the physical vehicle that our psyche inhabits. Evidence of this elemental level is seen in the solid or earth principle of the bones and other hardware in the body, the watery or fluid circulations, the airy or gaseous processes in the organism, and the fiery or radiant and electrical phenomena. All these levels of activity are elemental in principle, as matter and energy are absorbed, used and discharged in the life maintenance cycle. The body we were born with is not the one we shed at death. Very little is left of the original substance. Indeed, the bulk of what we have carried was only there for a relatively short time ranging from a few hours to a few years. Only some of the brain cells are said to live as long as the man, so that what is normally considered as the reliable base of most people's existence is in fact extremely ephemeral. Our bodies may contain enough iron for a nail, but it is in transit. Moreover, nothing in the world about us, even in the most apparently solid objects such as mountains, is permanent, because even if substances are in a chemically pure condition they are still disappearing and reappearing at the atomic level. Beyond this level lies the electronic world of pure Force and Form, and beyond this a void of Unmanifest Existence that mirrors the same reality found beyond the Keter of Azilut. This is one meaning of the expression 'Keter is in Malkhut and Malkhut is in Keter'.

Above the elemental level of existence is the vegetable level, based on the unit of the cell. The cell is an organic complex of atomic and molecular Force and Form, raised from an inorganic state into one of life. Cells may be simple or specialized, but all are based on the same model, which enables them to grow, to feed, to reproduce, and to die – that is to return the elements and energies involved in the life process to the inorganic level. On the lower face of Asiyyah, the cell occupies the key role, although it manifests in various ways. The great triad formed by Malkhut, Hod and Nezah constitutes the basic vegetable level, with Nezah as the active cycling principle, Hod as the passive adjusting system, and Malkhut as the material base of vegetable life. They are all connected by paths of membrane which enclose, respond and filter the processes going on within the cell. This great vegetable triad has at its centre Yesod, which is the coordinating Foundation for a relatively autonomic existence. Plants are governed by this triad, their energy and form maintained by the balance between the active and passive sefirot and the ground base of Malkhut. Yesod on the column of consciousness indicates an intelligence founded on rhythms and responses coming in on all the paths. The small triads that are composed of the paths focused on Yesod define the ability to respond, to move (if only to turn to the sun), and to process the energy and matter circulating through the organism. Even though we are human beings, we contain this plant level in that we grow, feed, reproduce and die. Anyone who lives by bread alone is in this position. He is a vegetable man, the lowest rung of the human condition.

The next level up is the animal. Expressed in the lower face of Asiyyah as the small triad of Hod-Nezah-Tiferet, the connection with the principle of a central nervous system enables the exercise of will. While this will may be primitive, it is nevertheless a higher level of consciousness and gives the animal a wider scope than the vegetable kingdom which is confined to very narrow limits. The world experienced through the central nervous system may be simple or complex, depending on the state of evolution of the creature. The sheep is infinitely more intelligent than the most hybrid rose, but it is stupid next to an ape, as an ape is to a man. In the case of the sheep and ape it is a question of sophistication in the nervous system. With the man comes something belonging to another World, or at least the potentiality of contacting a higher realm of consciousness. The difference of level is as much a quantum leap above the ape as the ape's level of experience is above the rose, and the rose's above the earth it grows in. The earth is the stone in Jacob's dream, at the base of a ladder stretching up to Heaven.

As a man can exist on the vegetable level of human existence, so can he in the purely animal. These levels on the Tree of man are seen in the upper face of Asiyyah. Here the vegetable and animal states are transposed into the simultaneous lower face of Yezirah, which is the autonomic part of the psyche.

The coincidence of upper Asiyyah and lower Yezirah explains the mechanics and state of natural man's psychological condition. Underlying his moods, as they oscillate between action and rest, are the biological rhythms. At one moment he desires excitement, at another peace. For a period he is full of vitality, and then he is depleted and bored. These states reflect the fluctuations between the active and the passive pillars of the whole Asiyyatic Tree, which includes the levels of physical, cellular, chemical and atomic balances expressed in its side triads. These side triads are synthesized in the central triads of organs, tissue, metabolism and electro-magnetic organism, all of which influence the ordinary psychological state of natural man, as simple day-to-day observation of oneself will show.

The vegetable level of our existence is ruled by the laws of eating and excreting, waking and sleep. We may or may not reproduce, but we are bound to the rhythms of food and activity and rest or we die – the final phase of the great cyclic law that governs organic life. There are many minor laws that fit into the main ones, such as breathing, which is eating and excreting the element of air. However, of significance to us is not just that natural man is subject to them, but that he is for the most part unaware that they govern his existence to such a degree that on this level he has little or no will of his own. This is an unacceptable statement to many people, but the fact is that the state of the vegetable man is the most common. Whole generations will live and die in one place, do much as their fathers and mothers did, have similar views of the world despite the spread of education. The parochial attitude of the village is not only found in the depths of the country but in the city, where millions wish to live a secure and regular life with minimal disturbance from outer and inner worlds.

The animal man is a different matter. Possessing some degree of will, he can, and often does, disturb the mass of vegetable people who work the fields, factories and offices that maintain the community. Such people as the Wright brothers, who persisted until they made a craft that would fly, have shaken and changed the world as much as any Hitler or Napoleon. The animal man possesses drive and perseverance; he has an objective beyond the pursuit of comfort and pleasure. He will defy pain and disappointment in order to obtain his objective, be it the conquest of an empire or the development of an idea. Such people abound in history, which records, not the accounts of the relatively placid masses, but the victories and achievements of individuals with a will of their own. In nature the most dominant of the species rules the herd, and while a leader may be subject to a higher cosmic power he nevertheless acts as the directing will in that community or field. Animal men are rare enough to stand out. They can usually be observed at the top of their professions, be it in commerce, science, art or government. Their hallmark is ambition and a sense of direction. This is what separates them from vegetable men, who may dream of remarkable achievements, but who choose the security of regular breadwinning to the high risk of failure in the fiercely competitive world of the animal man's jungle.

A fully developed natural man has reached the Keter of the Asiyyatic Tree. His psycho-biological organism contains all the sefirot, pillars, tirads and worlds of Asiyyah and the lower face of Yezirah. This means he has the mineral, vegetable and animal levels of potentiality actualized to the full, and as such he is a very powerful incarnate being. He is the Asiyyatic Adam, the spearhead of organic life on earth.

As the synthesis of all the earthly realms, he has dominion over the animals, plants and elements on our planet. However, while he remains only an Asiyyatic Adam he is confined to that realm to be born, live and die, in what many spiritual traditions describe as a Cyclic Existence. In Kabbalah this recycling of the Nefesh or natural soul is called the Gilgulim or the Wheels of Transmigration, which has a strong affinity with the Buddhist conception of the Wheel of Life. Under such a condition a person continually returns to incarnate existence until the task that soul is designed to perform is carried out or perfected on the natural level. The number of times, it is said, varies from many thousands to a handful or less. It is also possible, and again all traditions agree, to release oneself from the Wheel of carnal existence in one lifetime, or indeed, one moment of full realization that takes a man right up through all the Worlds into the presence of the Divine. Such an event may mean death on the physical level, but this is not invariably so, because it may be that the soul is required to perform, with Divine Consciousness, on the organic level. We have examples of this in the great world teachers. For less graced human beings, the path up Jacob's Ladder is slower, because to enter the upper Worlds suddenly and receive their full influx would be too much for the physical as well as the psychological organism. The Talmud tells the story of four rabbis who entered Paradise: one became mad, one died, another lost his faith, and only the last, Rabbi Akiba, came back in peace. This fable again stresses the importance of preparing a real foundation.

The first part of the preparation is a sound knowledge of the natural man's psyche. No one is born a Kabbalist. A man may have the potential, but he is, to begin with, a natural man. What memories he may have of where he came from soon fade in childhood as the psyche is more deeply enmeshed in carnal existence. There are of course those startling incidents of awakening, but these are reminders of things past and future as seen in the eternity of the present. The moments come and go, but they are meaningful only when the pleasures and pain of the natural condition become meaningless as the real purpose of life. Then, perhaps, in a state of disillusionment with the games of life, or even in the prospect of death, certain things are possible, because the situation is open to the upper levels. But we will come to this presently. First we must study the nature and structure of the natural man's psyche, and so begin a foundation in the next World of lower Eden.★

★ For a detailed account of the physical body and the Tree see the section 'The Body' in the author's *Adam and the Kabbalistic Tree*, Rider & Co., London, and Weiser, New York, 1974.

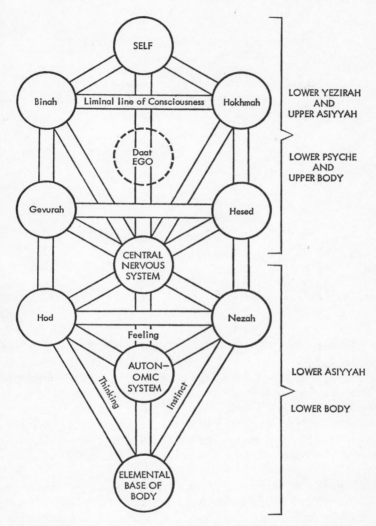

SELF

Binah

Liminal line of Consciousness

Hokhmah

LOWER YEZIRAH
AND
UPPER ASIYYAH

Daat
EGO

LOWER PSYCHE
AND
UPPER BODY

Gevurah

Hesed

CENTRAL
NERVOUS
SYSTEM

Hod

Nezah

Feeling

AUTON-
OMIC
SYSTEM

LOWER ASIYYAH

Thinking

Instinct

LOWER BODY

ELEMENTAL
BASE OF
BODY

Figure 10. Psycho-Biology of Man. *In this Asiyyatic Tree is shown the interleaving of psyche and body. The lower face generates in its cellular intelligence the three organic types, while the upper face, which is simultaneously the lower face of Yezirah, produces in its Daat, which is the Knowledge of the body, the ego, the Foundation of the psyche.*

6
Natural Adam: The Psyche

The great lower triangle of Asiyyah contains the three subtriads of muscles, organs and nerves. These generate what are known as the instinctive, feeling and thinking aspects of physical man. The instinctive triad is concerned mainly with practical matters. It is active and usually outwardly orientated. The feeling triad, balanced between the pillars, is introvert. Highly sensitive as the mediator to inner states, its function may be active or passive. The thinking triad operates in logic. Passive by nature, its concern is reflection and communication. Its orientation is mostly external.

In natural man, these triads work in an ever-adjusting combination, so that no matter what situation occurs one of the triads will deal with it: if a man walks, the instinctive triad is operative; if he has to assess somebody's mood, the feeling triad will inform him of their state; and if he has to solve a problem, his thinking triad will assemble all the pros and cons for calculation and decision.

In most natural men one of the triads predominates. This is due to the fact that no one's physical or psychological tree is in perfect balance. The imbalance may root back to the genes of one's parents, or to the particular temperament incarnated in one's body, or both, as nothing is separate in the universe. Either way, natural men and women tend to approach life principally through one triad. We recognize them as doers, feelers and thinkers. Indeed, certain professions may be classified by these body types. Sportsmen and soldiers, for instance, tend to be the instinctive type, artists and poets the feelers, and scientists and philosophers the thinking type. The classification must not be regarded as hierarchical, because all three types are equal. The mathematician may be as much a fool in the jungle as the musician is before a computer or the explorer in a concert hall. Each body type has remarkable gifts and facility, but all are biological in nature; they reflect the automatic processes of the vegetable level in man.

There is a direct connection between the three lower levels of Kabbalistic comprehension and the three body types. The literal approach is designed for the instinctive man of action, the allegorical for the person of feeling and the metaphysical method for the thinker. But the mystical experience is of a quite different order from that of natural intelligence. Its techniques will be dealt with later.

The upper face of Asiyyah is the simultaneous lower face of Yezirah. The sefirah at the centre of the complex is not only the Daat of Asiyyah, that is Knowledge of the body, but the Yesod of Yezirah, the Foundation of the psyche. Together they form the man's image of his body, and indeed some Kabbalists refer to this Daat/Yesod as the foundation of the Zelem or pre-existent Yeziratic shadow-vessel upon which the body is moulded and into which it grows on maturity. The Daat/Yesod focus on the central column of consciousness is natural man's psycho-biological organ of perception. From birth it is the instrument by which he experiences both himself and the outside world. The main function of this dual sefirah is to present data to the level of ordinary everyday consciousness. These can be images stimulated by the central or autonomic nervous systems below in the lower face of Asiyyah, such as signals coming from the eye, or images drawn from the unconscious that lies beyond the liminal line stretched between the Yeziratic Hod and Nezah above. In the normal conscious state the images are usually a mixture of outer and inner stimuli, but at night or in day-dreams they are mostly inner in origin. In Kabbalah, Yesod is called the non-luminous mirror.

The Yeziratic Yesod is the ordinary mind. It is the place where the influence of a person's home, education and attitudes to himself and the world manifest. Slowly built up since childhood, the Yeziratic Yesod accretes a structure of experience and criteria by which a man identifies himself. This picture, which is determined by many factors of temperament, place and fortune, becomes the ego.

The Greek word *ego* means 'I', and though it may appear as a single strong identity it is in fact composed of many smaller elements acquired over the years. Some of these elements work as a group, but in some cases they are quite contradictory or unconscious factors. The image that a man has of himself is often not the one his friends have of him.

Most people play different roles to meet domestic, social and professional situations. The roles, performed by a series of personalities that overlay the ego to protect it, are made up of acquired elements. Shielding the ego, the persona acts as a mask, which is what the word *persona* means in Latin. In Kabbalah the patriarch Joseph is ascribed to Yesod. He had a coat of many colours, which describes allegorically the composition of this sefirah. He was also the high servant of Pharaoh and the interpreter of dreams, which hints at Yesod's role and function.

Yesod is at the centre of four paths, three connected with the great lower triad and one called the path of the Zadek, or honest man, up to Tiferet. This makes a complex of four triads focused on the bio-psychological ego. The triads may be divided into lower and upper, or inner and outer. They may also be seen as active and passive according to the side pillar to which they are attached, so that there is an active and passive introvert and extrovert pair. They perform as interacting triads for any process flowing between the body and the psyche. Extremely complex in structure and dynamics, they enable Yesod to draw on the Trees above and below, be it to alert the central nervous system embodied in the Yeziratic Malkhut to unseen danger, fish out an old memory from the unconscious or allow a life-altering illumination into Yesodic vision. As the mental mechanics of the lower Yeziratic face, these triads are the intelligence of the natural man. While they are extraordinarily subtle and versatile they are not, in an un-developed person, to be compared with anything above Yesodic consciousness.

Beyond the threshold of the ordinary mind lies the Tiferet of Yezirah. Centre of many paths and midway point between the upper and lower faces of Yezirah, it is also the simultaneous Keter of Asiyyah, Crown of the body and heart of the psyche. It is aptly called the Seat of Solomon because of its unique position between the pillars of Mercy and Severity and the inner and outer parts of the psychological organism. From this position a man can see down eight paths, into at least eleven triads and three Worlds, because here also is the Malkhut of

Beriah. For natural man, this is the highest place he can reach under ordinary conditions. It is in this place that the unforgettable moments of a lifetime are perceived. How else could it be, because in this position we are suspended between Heaven and Earth.

The names given to this Tiferet are many. It is the luminous mirror to the non-luminous mirror of Yesod, which describes their relationship very precisely. It is called the Watcher; and all of us have experienced at some point in our lives that sense of observing events, or ourselves, as if from above. This is the Watchman often mentioned in the Bible. It is sometimes seen as a guardian angel; that part of oneself which guides one through highly complex situations with great skill, occasionally even saving one's foolish life. It is occasionally called the Guide. Modern Jungian psychologists name it the 'old wise man' within. It is known also by the title 'Heart of Hearts', and is said to contain the Presence of the Lord. In Kabbalah it is 'the Seat of Faith', the place where 'Thou' is found.

For natural man the Yeziratic Tiferet is the zenith of organic experience. As a vegetable and animal being he had a body and an identity which is at the centre of his Nefesh or vital soul. The identity in Yesod is the foundation of natural reality, but above this is dim awareness of something greater than the ego, something deeper, more real that comes into clear view in moments of intense danger, passion or stillness. This a man can recognize as his true Self. It is closer to what he essentially is than his ego, which in its presence is no more than a working mind dealing with everyday matters. To be in direct contact with one's real Self is quite memorable, even though a man may, and many do, try to bury it beneath ordinary living. The reason for retreating from such an experience is because Tiferet is the sefirah of Truth, and to have one's delusions and dreams exposed to its light can be very painful.

Tiferet is one's individuality. It is that incarnate Self common to all men, yet peculiar to each person. It is called Beauty, and not without reason: besides being the focus of an exquisite and marvellous symmetry of Force, Form and Will, it contains the place where God and man can consciously conjoin. Its other Kabbalistic name – Adornment – expresses its quality precisely: it is, and is not; it is to be seen, yet is not to be taken as the ultimate reality. Beauty is Truth and Truth is Beauty, yet neither is that which remains hidden by their very manifestation in the glass of the luminous mirror of the Self of Tiferet.

As the Crown of the organic Tree, Tiferet is the peak level of experience possible for vegetable and animal existence. In man there are further stages which he can realize while still embodied in the flesh: a realization which may be unconscious or conscious.

The liminal line defined by the path stretched from the Yeziratic Hod to Nezah is the normal threshold of consciousness between the ego and the Self. Its penetration fluctuates up and down the vertical 'path of the honest man', according to factors above and below the liminal line. This line is created by the psycho-biological functions of Hod and Nezah, which represent the voluntary and involuntary mental and organic processes.

While this pair of sefirot work the instinctive and mental mechanics in the lower face of Yezirah, there are two side sefirot above Tiferet that operate the emotional life of incarnate man. In the case of the natural person they are within the unconscious, that is well beyond the usual range of Yesodic awareness, although they have a powerful indirect influence on the person's life. They can come into consciousness only when a man is firmly established in Tiferet, and few natural men have accomplished this, despite their claims of being true to their Self. What Yesod believes about being master of fate is a sad illusion, as many lives, when honestly regarded, will reveal. Will is an attribute of the Self, and while it can be invoked in times of crisis it is rarely sustained, and Yesod soon clouds over the clarity and decision born at the dramatic moment.

The Gevurah and Hesed of Yezirah are the outer and inner aspects of emotion. Judgement on the pillar of Form is passive and responsive, and Mercy on the pillar of Force is active and initiating. Together they balance and control the emotional life, be it conscious or unconscious. They can be seen as the moral qualities of a man, the integrity, the capacity for love and courage. Here is the soul of a person. It is the triad where charity and discrimination abide. Focused on the Self, the contraction of Judgement contains the excessive expansion of Mercy, which in turn opens out the strictness of Judgement. Below and to each side are the storehouse triads of active and passive emotional complexes that connect both to the Self and the instinctive and mental sefirot of Nezah and Hod. Hesed and Gevurah, and their adjacent paths, affect a man's emotional life: from beyond the hidden Tiferet, they influence the mind of Yesod to create moods.

Above the outer emotion that holds us in check and the inner emotion that provides enormous psychological power, are the twin sefirot of the intellect, Binah and Hokhmah. Placed also on the passive and active columns, they perform the functions of Understanding and Wisdom. Understanding is the reflective and formulating side, not of the mental gymnastics of Hod, which is an informative and communicating principle, but of real and profound intellect concerned with first principles. Understanding acts, like Judgement to Mercy on the emotional level, as a counterbalance to Wisdom, which has the active power of revelation. Understanding likewise needs Wisdom to stop it from formulating an idea into rigid dogma. Defined in man as outer and inner intellect, they both represent deepest thought. Experience of this level is very rare in natural man, as is the level of real emotion. Most people take their everyday thoughts and feelings as intellect and emotion, but these are often only the mechanical products of Hod, Nezah and the surrounding triads. There are natural men who experience directly the upper levels of emotion and intellect, and such events provoke great discoveries or works of art. But this tends to happen only a few times in a lifetime, and the person lives on the laurels of a dream of what he saw through the gates of Paradise. To sustain the position and gain permanent entrance into the upper Worlds one has to become a supernatural man.

In natural man the upper reaches of the psyche are deep within the unconscious, beyond the Self. Centred on the ego of Yesod, the radius of the personal consciousness stretches in a circle from the Malkhut of Yezirah, that is the central nervous system of the body's Tiferet, round each of the dual psycho-biological sefirot of Hod and Nezah, to the Watcher of the Yeziratic Tiferet. This is the extreme range of the mind in its ordinary daytime state. At night the body consciousness slips down to focus principally on the central nervous system, the Watcher of the body. The next orbit of consciousness is centred on the Self: its range extends down to the ego and encloses the two instinctive and emotional pairs of sefirot. Its upper reaches enclose the non-sefirah of the Yeziratic Daat, that is Knowledge of quite a different World to that experienced under normal earth conditions. This sphere in natural man is called the Individual Unconscious and relates to all those experiences that have passed through the ego of Yesod and into the psyche to attach themselves to the sefirot, paths and triads surrounding the Self (see Fig. 11).

Deeper still, and focused on the Daat of Yezirah, is a radius of the unconscious that is connected with all men that have lived, are living and will live. Tradition places the Great Mother and Father at the head of the two outer pillars, and these, with Gevurah and Hesed, the sefirot

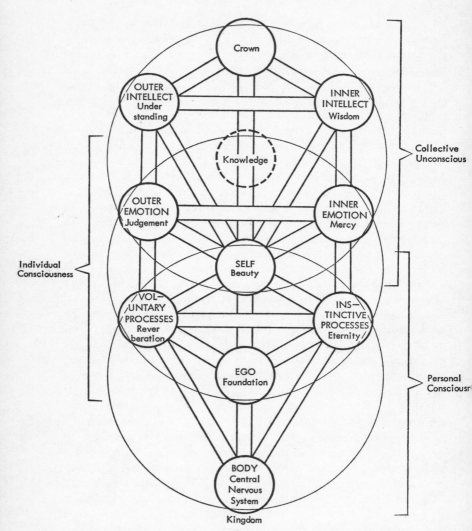

Figure 11. Psyche. *The psyche like the body has an anatomy which may be set out on the Tree. In this yeziratic scheme the active and passive functions of intellect, emotion and instinctive intelligence flank the central column of consciousness. The circles indicate the spheres of influence of the various levels of awareness and inherent knoweldge.*

of emotion, help to compose the race memory inherent in all human beings. The connection is made at the lowest point with the Self and at the highest with the Keter of Yezirah, which is the simultaneous Tiferet of Beriah, the realm of the spirit. The scale of this radius of consciousness is cosmic, and for the vast majority of humanity totally hidden within the deep of the Collective Unconscious this level is the bridge between Man and the Divine.

As will be observed, all the orbits of influence interleave, so that a natural man is by no means cut off from the source of his being. The chief spiritual difficulty is that he is unconscious of the influxes descending through his nature. He need not remain unconscious of them, but that is often his choice. As a fully developed natural man a person can command the animal, vegetable and mineral kingdoms below him, and yet not have dominion over himself, for despite the glimpses he may have into Paradise and even Heaven, he may be too egocentric to notice, or be too useful to the Earth, which will utilize his power for the planet's purpose.

To become free of natural law, to escape the Gilgulim of birth, life and death, a natural man must become supernatural, transform the unconscious into the conscious and rise beyond the terrestrial Keter of Asiyyah, even though his body may be still subject to organic rule. To do this he must submit his will, commit himself to escape from mundane slavery, known in Kabbalah as bondage in Egypt.*

*For a detailed account of the psyche see section 'Psyche' in the author's *Adam and the Kabbalistic Tree*, Rider & Co., London, and Weiser, New York, 1974.

7
Slaves in Egypt

We have seen in the last two chapters how natural man exists consciously in one and a half Worlds; his body occupying the whole Tree of Asiyyah and his ordinary ego mind the lower face of Yezirah. The other Worlds are present within his being, but they are unrealized, and act as unconscious influences over his life. To the average natural man the idea that he is ruled by unperceived forces either never enters his mind or is an unacceptable premise. While he appreciates and respects the powers and materiality of the Asiyyatic World, he for the most part dismisses the notion of the supernatural. I say for the most part, because there is in him an inherent memory of a remote past, a suspicion of there being more to the present than is seen, and a deep apprehension of what lies beyond the future. To the physically orientated ego mind the supernatural is a threat, because it undermines the foundation of its very existence, making what is solid insubstantial and what is permanent ephemeral. One moment's glimpse of Eternity can cause the most ancient mountain to vanish into timelessness, and this is not a pleasant experience to have, if one believes, as the ego often does, that it is special, if not immortal. Few natural men can face the idea of their own death. It may happen to others but not to oneself; at least not today – and tomorrow never comes. Such Yesodic illusion is the ego's screen against any other reality.

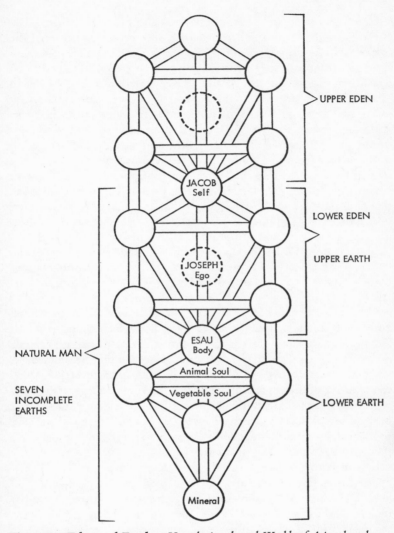

UPPER EDEN

LOWER EDEN

UPPER EARTH

JACOB
Self

JOSEPH
Ego

ESAU
Body

Animal Soul

Vegetable Soul

NATURAL MAN

SEVEN
INCOMPLETE
EARTHS

LOWER EARTH

Mineral

Figure 12. Eden and Earth. *Here the interleaved Worlds of Asiyyah and Yezirah describe the estate of natural man. Below, in the lowest face, are the incomplete Worlds which lack the perfection inherent in the full Tree of Man. Esau the symbol of earthly humanity is placed at the centre of the physical Tree. Joseph, the honoured servant of Pharaoh is halfway between body–slave and master–man, represented by his father Jacob, who in becoming Israel converted the upper face of Earth into the lower face of Eden.*

How did this situation of unconsciousness in man come about? The Bible has it that Adam fell from Grace, that he descended from the upper Worlds of the spirit into the lower World of matter. In Kabbalistic terms this can be translated as slipping down Jacob's Ladder the distance of one face, so that Adam, whose natural habitat was Eden or Yezirah, was incarnated in the flesh of the lower face of Asiyyah. There are many versions of the Fall, with as many explanations for its happening. Some Kabbalists describe it as a malfunction of the sefirot during the unfolding of the Worlds; others, as the inevitable separation of the created from its Creator. Yet others see Adam's situation as that of a prince sent out into the lower Worlds by his father in order to experience the kingdom he will eventually rule. Certain Kabbalists say that God put Adam in this position so that he might have the pleasure of helping him. And not a few others claim that Man, in Asiyyah, is the fleshly manifestation of the Azilutic, Adam and that through this earthly creature God may have direct access and appreciation of the lower Worlds. I myself subscribe to this notion, and to the concept that each individual is incarnated in Asiyyah in order to perform a particular task as indicated by his talents and path in life.

On birth the psychological or Yeziratic body of an individual becomes firmly attached to the Asiyyatic body. The connection was first made at the Keter of Asiyyah (the simultaneous Tiferet of Yezirah), the process being continued down the octave Lightning Flash through the stages of father (Hokhmah), mother (Binah), conception (Daat), cell multiplication (Hesed), cell differentiation (Gevurah), to the establishing of a Yeziratic Malkhut in the Tiferet of the body, that is, the central nervous system. The lower face is completed in the organism by being brought into working order and tune by Nezah and Hod, so that after the last interval of Yesod, the autonomic system takes over, once the baby's Malkhutian body is severed from its mother.*

The lower face of the Asiyyatic Tree is tissue, organs, muscles and nerves. Having no direct interleaving with the Yeziratic or any other upper World it is in a sense incomplete. In Kabbalah the term 'Incomplete Worlds' refers to those existences that were created before the present one. They collapsed, we are told, because they were either unstable, being too much on one pillar or the other, or because they lacked the full power of the Holy Spirit. When the present universe was established the remnants of six of the incomplete worlds were

---

* See the detailed account of the gestation process in Chapter 16 of the author's *Tree of Life*, Rider & Co., London, and Weiser, New York, 1972.

incorporated into the lower part of the general evolutionary scheme. They were called the kingdoms of Edom. The seventh kingdom of Tebel was almost perfect, so it became the model of incarnate Adam, known to us as a human being. There were, however, fragments of the earlier Worlds that remained outside the final World system, and these, tradition says, generated evil, that is the demonic or unbalanced forces and forms that lie beyond the outer pillars and below the incomplete kingdoms of Edom.

The tree of Asiyyah without its Yeziratic connections may be considered as the seven incomplete Earths, and indeed its terrestrial limitation is well defined at physical death when mineral or chemical metabolism ceases and life departs from the vegetable and animal body. At such a moment the Nefesh or vital soul separates from the upper face of Yezirah or the bottom half of the psyche. As would be expected, the lower part of the Asiyyatic body then collapses, decays and diffuses back into its various earth-bound levels of energy, matter and elemental consciousness.

In Kabbalistic tradition these Seven Earths of Asiyyah also represent seven layers of terrestrial existence or levels up the central column of the Asiyyatic Tree. They are sometimes called countries and have names, the lowest one Malkhut being Eretz or Land. These countries have inhabitants each of which has its being at a particular state of consciousness. They are actually described as being situated one over the other, so that they may occupy the same Tree or place, but in quite different ways. Thus to take a simple parallel, bacteria and a man's psyche may live in the same body but they are aware of quite different levels. From this Kabbalistic view the bacteria that occupy the lower face of the Asiyyatic Tree has little direct relationship with the upper Worlds. Indeed it can be said that the mineral, vegetable and animal levels of experience being almost entirely confined to Asiyyah are in this sense imperfect. Only man who can transform his state and so convert the upper face of Asiyyah into the lower face of Yezirah can be considered a complete earth being. However, as observed, most men prefer to have their conscious centre of gravity in the vegetable kingdom and live in the human equivalent. In this condition they experience the travail of the lower face of Asiyyah without realizing there is even an upper face or Earth counterpart, not to mention the Terrestrial Eden that interleaves with it. This was the situation of the Israelite slaves in Egypt.

The Bible tells us that Jacob went down into Egypt with seventy souls. That is, he descended from Canaan or Yezirah with the seven sefirot of construction (each sefirah has ten small sefirot of its own) into Asiyyah or Egypt where he dwelt. In Hebrew the word for Egypt is Mitzriaim whose root means 'constriction' or 'confinement'. At first things went well for the Israelites because Joseph, Jacob's son, was viceroy of Egypt and Pharaoh's good servant. In Kabbalistic terms Jacob, the Self, is the Tiferet of Yezirah and the Keter of Asiyyah; and Joseph, or ego, is the Yesod of Yezirah and the Daat of Asiyyah, which demonstrates their roles and relationships and why it worked well when they were present in Egypt. In time Jacob died and he was taken back *up* to be buried in Canaan or Yezirah, while his spirit returned to the bosom of his forefathers in Beriah. Later Joseph also died, and was gathered to his fathers, but his body was kept mummified *down* in Egypt until the Israelites rose up out of Egypt and went to Canaan. We have here in allegory natural man's situation after he has spent some time in Asiyyah. From birth until youth he has innocence, integrity and a sense of truth, but this is often lost or at least buried beneath the pleasures and pains of the flesh. In time he forgets the upper country from which he came. The memories fade, or are rather blurred by the activities of Asiyyatic life. Desire, survival and comfort become more important than anything else. The momentary glimpses into Paradise of early years become less and less, as life's responsibility grows, until they are regarded as dreams and fantasies of childhood. By the time retirement and old age have come it is too late to do anything before he is drawn by death back into the cycle again. This is the Gilgul or Wheel of Slavery. Totally ruled by the laws of the elements and organic nature man is confined to the Lower Earth of Egypt. It is true that the ego still rules as viceroy over the land, but it is now only an empty coat of many colours, which for lack of the guide of the Self believes it is Pharaoh, the God-King.

However not all the Children of Israel wish to be slaves. There are some who still retain a dim memory of where they came from and listen to the tale repeated to every generation of a promise made to their forefathers about a far country flowing with milk and honey. To most of the Israelites it is a children's story full of marvellous but quite unbelievable things. Present existence is the only reality, they say, and that is enough to contend with, without contemplating a journey into the unknown. To those who listen carefully to the story it gradually becomes apparent that it is no infantile fantasy, but a precise history and method of action, devotion and contemplation whose real message is how to escape from slavery. For those prepared to take up the option, many things become possible; for Heaven, alerted to an awakening Adam, sets Providence in motion down throughout the Worlds to assist them rise, so that they can enter, even while embodied in Asiyyah, the lower Garden of Eden.

8
The Promised Land

The feeling of isolation is common to everyone. Indeed this sense of separation is one of the main driving forces in life. It brings men and women together, begets families and generates tribes and nations where people feel they belong. But, as everybody knows, even in the most intimate of personal relationships one is alone; and one is yet more so in a group, however large. This sense of isolation does not come from nature. If it did it could easily be resolved in the identity of the herd. No, the cause is elsewhere. It is the separation from the Worlds above which afflicts us while we live only in the incomplete realms of Asiyyah.

The feeling of being out of place in the natural world is found in all cultures and times. An old American folksong expresses it well in the words: 'I'm just a poor wayfaring stranger a-travelling through this world of woe. But I have no fear of toil or danger in that fair land to which I go.' In the Bible the same idea is seen in the symbol of the Exile and the Promised Land. Perceived literally, men have regarded the Exile from and regaining of the Holy Land as an historical event. The Christians and Arabs fought over the possession of Palestine in the Middle Ages, and today the Israelis, after two thousand years of exile, are still fighting to maintain their foothold on Zion. While the significance of this small Levantine country is great to three of the world's major religions, its real meaning is often forgotten. Zion is the Holy Mountain, and on its top is the heavenly Jerusalem. This indicates that although the Promised Land may have its base in Malkhut, like the pillow stone at the foot of Jacob's Ladder, the true Holy Land by definition is situated in another World. The notion of a far and ideal country is also found all over the world in folklore and myth. Some peoples see the Promised Land as beyond the sky, others over the mountains, across the sea and even at the end of the rainbow. It is always in a place other than here; although natural men invariably see it in physical terms: something to be discovered or worked for, like El Dorado or Utopia. Perhaps the most modern version of the myth is the hidden valley of Shangri-La in the Himalayas, but even this is still set in Asiyyah.

In Kabbalah the Promised Land lies beyond the Tiferet of Yezirah, the Self of the psychological Tree. It begins just above Tebel, the uppermost of the Seven Earths, which can be defined as the supernal triad of Asiyyah or the simultaneous Hod-Nezah-Tiferet triad of Yezirah. In psychological terms this complex is known as Awakening Consciousness. It is also known as the Triad of Hope.

Stories of glimpses into the Promised Land abound in world folklore although often in a watered down and distorted form. Jack and the Beanstalk is an example. Here a boy (i.e. an incomplete or natural man) climbs up a magic beanstalk and enters into an upper World. Not unnaturally everything appears larger than life and somewhat frightening, hence the symbol of the giant. His own rapid descent and cutting of the link of the beanstalk shows his decision to live in the safety of the natural world below. The tale of Aladdin is another version of natural man's encounter with the upper Worlds, and so is that of Cinderella. This last gives a detailed account of the powers and Worlds involved. Cinderella, the rightful heiress (or soul) of her father's house, is made to live in the kitchen (the body) while her stepmother's (ego's) ugly daughters (personas) usurp her place. However, with the aid of her fairy godmother (a teacher), a pumpkin (the vegetable soul) and some mice (the animal soul) are transformed into a coach and horses (Ezekiel's Merkabah or chariot) which will convey Cinderella to the ball (the next World). Her rags are also changed into a fabulous gown (she shifts from the natural to the supernatural). In this state of Grace she is raised from Asiyyah up into Yezirah, where she meets the prince (spirit

c

of Beriah). After various difficulties with the claims of ego and the personas, the soul and the spirit are united in marriage, much to the pleasure of the king (Adam Kadmon of Azilut).

Such folktales are obviously not conceived by ordinary storytellers. In Kabbalah there is a tradition that there are thirty-six Just Men or Zadekim in the world at any one time. This idea of a hidden company of wise and powerful persons is again common to all cultures and is often expressed in folktales as the mysterious stranger who turns up at a crucial time in the hero's journey. Usually unrecognized at first, the magician or fairy godmother intervenes to enable the mission to be completed. The parallel in spiritual progress is precise, even to the master being recognized only when the disciple is ready. This gives us a strong clue as to what calibre of men wrote the original tales, why they were written and whom they were aimed at.

The function of the hidden Zadekim is vital to humanity. They are the Teachers or Maggidim, whose task is to aid those men and women who wish to evolve spiritually. However, this cannot be accomplished directly for natural man does not normally recognize the presence of such highly evolved beings, because they appear as quite ordinary people. This fact makes things both difficult and easy. Easy because a hidden Zadek can be right in the middle of life without being noticed, and difficult because he can only help people who recognize him and their own need for help. Only then can he reveal himself. Every spiritual tradition has such people. One can meet a Sufi antique dealer or a Kabbalist accountant without knowing it, although they may quickly recognize each other, as two people awake in a dormitory might. The number of Zadekim is certainly more than thirty-six, although the thirty-six may well occupy a special level in the spiritual company which is sometimes called the Inner Circle of humanity.

While the Zadekim of a Tradition may scatter their teaching stories, and hints and traces of their presence and work, throughout the World of Asiyyah, nothing can be done for a man until he comes to a decision to do something.

When moments of visionary insight occur, in quiet or in crisis, they make the person reflect that there is more to existence than the physical activities of eating, begetting and achieving ascendancy for a day before declining into retirement and death. Most people can recall these inner events with great clarity. It was as if they had intruded into another World – and indeed they had. The impact of this experience both thrills and frightens natural man, like Jack on the beanstalk, because it places him in a position where he has to go further into that new World or retreat. Most draw back, because they prefer the world they know, with its pain and toil, to the unknown, however promising it might be. Often the rejection of the Paradise side (the Yeziratic aspect) of the upper face of Asiyyah is violent, because it is not only new but threatens the status of the ego situated on the Earth side of the face. To lose the identity of the ego is unbearable for most people, because, as the Asiyyatic Daat, it is their only knowledge of physical reality. To earth-orientated beings the idea of letting go of the natural world is too much. This is the point of the Bible story of Jacob and Esau. Esau, the elder brother, sold his birthright to Jacob for a mess of pottage because he was sensually hungry. In doing so he lost his chance of spiritual possibility. He remained below in the natural world to become the father of the kings of Edom, or Asiyyah before there were kings in Israel. The kings of Edom represent in this context the seven incomplete stages before the Kingdom of Israel was established in the upper Worlds; the House of Israel is the Kabbalistic name of the Inner Circle of humanity.

When a natural man or woman decides to penetrate more deeply into the World that lies beyond Edom, Providence opens doors that were not only closed, but unseen by the natural eye. Suddenly, folk stories begin to come true, and the Bible transforms from the past into the present. It is then that Teshuvah, or the return home to the Promised Land, begins. Teshuvah is a Hebrew word that can mean 'repentance' or 'conversion'. In Kabbalistic terms it describes the release from the curse of Adam (that of working the Earth), and the transformation of the upper face of any lower World into the lower face of an upper. However, before the Exodus from Egypt can begin certain preconditions have to be met. When man is discontented enough seriously to want to give up his bondage he must be trained. At this point a spiritual teacher or maggid will usually appear. This happened to the Children of Israel in the person of Moses; it is the same in the life of an individual.

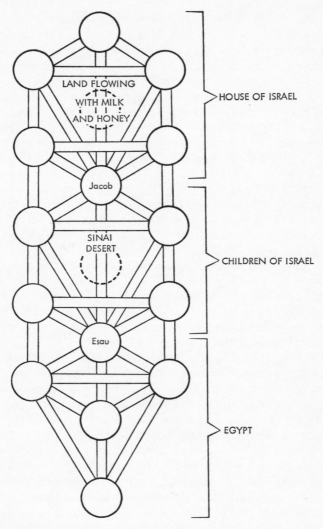

Figure 13. Bondage. *This pair of interleaved Trees shows the precise relationship between the states possible for evolving Man described in Genesis and Exodus. The going out of Egypt is seen here as the rising up out of bondage of lower Asiyyah into the desert between Egypt and the Promised Land. Sinai is the place where old slave habits must die and a new generation or Foundation be formed before one may enter the House of Israel, or the land flowing with milk and honey.*

9
Jacob and Esau

Esau and Jacob were twin brothers; that is two aspects of the same thing. Esau not only sold his birthright but also lost the blessing of his father and married a heathen woman. By these three events he gave up his place in the Land promised in the Covenant between his fore-fathers and God, where he and his descendants might have lived for ever. So he forfeited immortality and dwelt to the south below Israel in the Land of Edom, which means 'red', the colour of blood, in the kingdom of animal men. This place is also called the wilder-ness.

Jacob, the younger twin, succeeded Esau because he perceived the value of the birthright, and with the aid of his mother obtained the blessing of the firstborn. Thus he converted the upper face of Asiyyah into the lower face of Yezirah. This is the beginning of the process of Teshuvah or redemption. Esau, the unconverted and the unrepentant, remained as the Tiferet of Asiyyah while Jacob rose to become the Asiyyatic Keter or firstborn. Later, after wrestling with the angel of God, Jacob was renamed Israel. This was another conversion or rise in level, bringing the Keter of Asiyyah and the simultaneous Tiferet of Yezirah into contact with the Malkhut of Beriah which occupies the same place. At this point the second birth, or development of the soul out of the physical body of Asiyyah begins. It is in the face, below Jacob and above Esau, that the Children of Israel are found.

The name 'Children of Israel' is a very precise Kabbalistic term. It does not apply merely to people of Hebrew extraction, but defines a state of being above the animal level of Edom and that of total slavery in Egypt, but below the upper face of Yezirah, known as the entrance to the Holy Land, or, in this context, the House of Israel. Born as a natural man under the laws of Asiyyah, or in Sin, as some later Kabbalists call it, everyone on Earth begins as a child of Israel.

In childhood and youth the presence of another World is often sensed; or it occurs at least once in a moment of profound wonder at nature or the vast deep of the sky. There comes a time, however, when the Asiyyatic World requires its payment for services rendered; for everything in the Universe, including spiritual development, has to be paid for. In Asiyyah it is Adam's labour on the Earth and Eve's bearing of the next generation. When this debt is met the child (or natural man) becomes an adult and can move on to the next World. This move, alas, is not usually made. The Children of Israel soon forget, in the cares of the mundane world, the memory of that other reality. They lose sight of the promise given to their forefathers, and sell their birthright for mineral possessions, vegetable comfort and animal status. Like Esau, they forgo the blessing of the Father and marry an unbeliever: they not only turn away from their origin but cease to believe that it ever existed. Thus they become at worst vegetable slaves in Egypt, at best the Children of Esau dwelling in the Edom of animal men.

Those who remain Children of Israel, who retain some connection, however tenuous, with the upper Worlds from which they came, do not have an easy time either. Living in Edom and Egypt is difficult, because everyone about them is not only totally involved in the activities of Asiyyah, but regards them as outsiders, as lazy and as even dangerous. Firstly because, as one Kabbalist put it, 'the children of this World have more wisdom in their way than the children of Light', and secondly because the endless questioning of the value of physical existence is a direct threat to Esau's religion. The problem of the Child of Israel is that he participates in two Worlds. He cannot gain satisfaction, as Esau's children do, in pure Asiyyah; and he does not know how to enter and stay in the Paradise of Yezirah. He is considered abnormal by the mundane world, because of his lack of desire or interest in possessions or status; his own family often does not understand him.

Frequently he is chided for having no worldly ambition, and to talk about a higher World arouses an anger deeper than any animal passion because it places in jeopardy the whole philosophy of natural man's life.

Buried in the natural man's unconscious is a recognition of the upper Worlds that have been denied; and this is painful. Esau's resentment at losing his place is still present even though it was his own choice. Doggedly he clings to the rationalized security of the senses, forcing himself to believe in the reality of something that fades continually before his eyes. The Child of Israel angers him because he reminds him continually that everything of the Earth must pass, that the ego's illusion of its own importance is false, that even with each new birth the promise of youth must decay into death. This is the sorrow of Adam and Eve, and it is unbearable to look upon too closely or deeply. In their own defence, the Children of Esau at first ridicule the Children of Israel. Questions about the meaning of life and the search for something that will last for ever are considered unrealistic and of no use in a world governed by gain and loss, tooth and claw. 'Then why maintain the religion of our fathers?' asks the Child of Israel, observing the myriad temples in Edom and Egypt. 'Because it is tradition,' is the reply. 'But,' counters Israel's Child – and this has happened in every generation – 'You do not practise the precepts. You are hypocrites.' At this point the Children of Esau often become violent, especially those who claim to be the priests and preservers of their fathers' religion. They turn upon the questioners and the seekers after the truth, and drive them out of their community. And so it is that Jacob and Esau, brothers in blood, cannot live together, nor can they, even when reconciled, exist in the same country. Jacob has to go his own way (Genesis 33).

Jacob is the outsider, the stranger. Indeed, one of the root meanings of the word 'Hebrew' means just this. And Abram became an outsider, a stranger to his own father who was an idol-maker by profession. In Genesis 12, 'The Lord had said unto Abram, Get thee out of thy country, and from thy kindred, and from thy father's house, unto a land that I will show thee.'

After Jacob had made his choice he was sent out from his natural home with virtually nothing into a hostile country. Such is the situation of the Child of Israel. It is true he has his parents' blessing; that is, the archetypal influence from Hokhmah and Binah, the sefirot of Adam and Eve, or Wisdom and Understanding. But these are often only in the form of stories or ideas he only half comprehends. He knows that he can no longer live in, or be subject to the laws of Edom, but he does not know how to leave the country. Desperately he seeks a way out, calling upon God for help as the original Children of Israel did when in bondage in Egypt. Occasionally his loneliness and self-suspected madness are alleviated by a glimpse into Paradise, so that for a moment the upper face of Asiyyah or Earth, when transformed into the lower Eden, confirms his belief that the Promised Land actually exists. He desires more and more to enter that higher reality, but he has no command over the experience which can occur equally in times of joy or deep melancholy. He seeks a key, a door, any way to gain entrance. Some seekers try drugs. These open a window on to a world that is different from Asiyyah, but it has distorting panes and its glass is clouded by psychological impurities which give a view that has no comparison to the clarity of a moment of Grace. Kabbalistically the drug approach is seen to be not only spiritually illegitimate, but dangerous. Such expeditions may convince the naive that there is a next World, but they are only images in the mirror of the ego mind whose surface can be fractured for ever by chemical abuse, thus destroying its vital property as the non-luminous reflector of real illumination. The destruction of the Yeziratic Yesod and the Daat of the body is no light matter. It can burn a person's birthright out of his body leaving him with only a faint after-image memory of what might have been.

For the Child of Israel who seeks the traditional and legitimate ways it is a long and lonely business. He reads and studies the texts and scriptures, takes up various practices, performs prayers and meditations. But on his own, surrounded by people who consider him odd, his ability to sustain effort is erratic and often short-lived. He needs others to talk to, exchange and compare notes, but there is no one about: none that can even understand an inkling of his problem or the World he wishes to explore. Constantly he finds clues, but it is like half hearing a conversation from another room. He knows, yet he does not know what he knows. He sees, yet he cannot see clearly enough to remember what he once saw with such certainty. Books and practices indicate, yet do not tell, although they reveal more than he can comprehend. They are not enough. He needs help. He cannot do it all himself. His spiritual conceit is slowly dissolved. He sees he is not superior to Esau's Children. He is as they are. The only difference is that he is aware that he is different.

He is still a natural man, for all his yearning and insight and promise. To desire is not the same as to be able to perform, and it soon becomes obvious that he cannot remain what he is and enter the next World. A change is needed. A conversion, a real step towards redemption, is required, although he may not know at the time this is what it means. At such a crisis point, when often all the work and sacrifice seem to have been in vain, Providence usually organizes an apparently fortuitous meeting with someone who has a connection with a living Tradition. It may be one of the thirty-six Just Men, or even a Buddha or a Mohammed, but it is more likely to be a person at the very foot of the ladder of teachers, someone just one step up from the outsider, who knows enough to recognize his state and need. This meeting may have taken years to bring about, the elder watching the younger until he was ready for Kabbalah, which means 'to receive' the Tradition.

10
The Zadek

A Zadek is a just or saintly man. Zadekim are not born but made, partly by the assistance of God and partly by their own effort. No one becomes a Zadek against his will or is chosen. He chooses himself. By virtue of his own decision, he makes himself one of the Elect of Mankind. There are many who are called, but not chosen. That is, they do not select themselves to be worthy of the responsibilities of the task. Sometimes people wrongly believe they have been chosen and act out their lives according to what seems, to them, a divine mission. Such people often not only ruin their own progress but mar that of others. However even these spiritual disasters have their purpose in warning pilgrims what not to do.

A Zadek is a person who has taken on the responsibility of being an adult. He is himself, his own man, like the best of Esau's children who attain the level of Keter of Asiyyah. Full natural men however wish to go no further. They are content to be the rulers of the World below rather than servants of the World above. There are of course rare exceptions, when a full Esau, a great worldly man, will suddenly give up all he has and turn towards God. Indeed a wholehearted reprobate sometimes has more chance to enter the Kingdom of Heaven than a half-hearted saint, for he at least knows himself and how to commit and direct his will.

The act of directing the will is the first lesson the aspirant has to learn, because, as he has no doubt realized, he has no capacity to concentrate in one direction for any real length of time. The reason for this is that, while the Asiyyatic body Tree is well organized and aimed at organic balance, the Yeziratic Tree of the psyche is not. Natural men can live quite well in Asiyyah with the minimal operation of mental mechanics. In fact he can exist with the higher functions of the brain out of commission through disease or accidental damage. However, for someone wishing to live in the World above the animal and vegetable state of man, there is no organization and no foundation by which he can even gain a foothold. The sense of how difficult it is to grasp a new concept can be seen in the ordinary education of the Yesodic ego-mind. How much more subtle instruction must be needed to form a Foundation in the next World of Beriah. This is why only rare men can educate themselves in a balanced way into being a Zadek. A spiritual teacher is needed, who has himself passed through the same path. The best teachers are usually those who have just attained the next stage up. The instruction of the person just below them is one method of paying their debt to their own maggid or Teacher.

In Kabbalah the path between the ego-Yesod and the Tiferet of the Self in the Yeziratic Tree of the psyche is known as the Zadek path, after the Hebrew letter ascribed to it. The root of the letter Tsade, besides meaning 'honesty', also underlies the word for 'he who lies in wait'. The reason for the first is obvious in the relationship between the clear brightness of the Truth in the sefirah of Beauty and the non-luminous reflection of the sefirah of Foundation. The symbol of the sun and moon is sometimes used for Tiferet and Yesod to demonstrate their relationship. The second name of the path 'He who lies in wait' derives from the placing on the Tree of the twenty-two letters of the Hebrew alphabet, one for each of the twenty-two paths. Following the Lightning Flash sequence the letter Tsade fills the path between the ego and the Self. This path may be open or closed depending on whether Tiferet or Yesod is the seat of consciousness. Thus when Yesod is in command, the ego rules the natural state of rhythmic thoughts, feelings and actions, and when Tiferet is dominant a higher state of awareness, often described as 'looking down on oneself' occurs. This condition of awakening consciousness is the prelude to a state of Grace or a glimpse into Paradise.

The aspect of 'He who lies in wait' may be seen in two ways. One as the manifestation of one's personal devil, who resides in the dark side of the ego, and the other as the inner Zadek who reminds one to wake up, if only just in time. One might call these good and bad aspects as one's personal Jekyll and Hyde. They are quite different from the angels of good and evil who exist higher up the Tree to teach and tempt. The struggle between these emotional angels only occurs consciously when the person has reached a point where he really knows good from evil. At the level of the Zadek path this is not the issue, because the person is not yet awake enough to be fully capable of handling that stage. It is also another reason why the disciple needs help from a maggid. As in the folktales, the path into the unknown country is very hazardous. The hero, however brave, needs a guide.

One of the initial hazards of inexperience is that the seeker may meet a man who either believes mistakenly that he is a Zadek and Teacher, or has been one and has plans of his own. The man who believes he is a Zadek is eventually exposed as an imposter, because, although he has read all the books, or copies someone he suspects of being the authentic thing, he himself cannot produce real changes either in a disciple or in himself. His hints are sham, and the seeker soon leaves him with his illusions. Of greater danger is the man who has reached some level of realization. His quality is usually enigmatic, and he often possesses remarkable powers which he uses to intrigue and manipulate people who are not so evolved as himself. History is full of such men, whose influence has swayed large numbers of people, as did Sabbatai Zevi in the seventeenth century. He was a remarkable man, well acquainted with Kabbalah, who used its knowledge to persuade a whole community of Jews that he was the Messiah. He, like all who abuse the Teaching, eventually fell into the abyss of his own making. Alas, such men have the ability to fascinate and imprison people by their personal charisma, which is the exact reverse of Kabbalah, whose object is to free men from bondage. For this reason it is forbidden for the Kabbalist to practise the exercise of power over other people against their wills.

The tendency of taking the Teaching, or indeed anything, personally is the mark of the false Zadek. While he may have at one time been under instruction, perhaps been a model disciple, the initiation of submitting the will can often make a man back away from commitment at the last moment. Such a man can leave the Zadek path and descend to the ego, where he exercises all the powers and skills he has acquired, nominally for the sake of spiritual work, but in actuality for the glorification of his Yesodic image. To such people the image of themselves is most important, and with it come clothes and mannerisms, all of which suggest that they know about the next and the upper World. This role may be played in both orthodox and unorthodox forms. One may meet it in a magician or a rabbi, in the leader of a psychological group, and even in a priest of eminent lineage. The phenomenon occurs on the edge of all Traditions, and is one of the reasons for having a chain of Zadekim to watch over each other. Temptation is possible all the way up Jacob's Ladder. Lucifer was among the highest of archangels before he fell. Only God is perfect.

To come in contact with a dark or fallen Teacher is often part of a seeker's training. Many dead ends will present themselves; but all will teach him something, if only that others have trodden the Way before, or how to extract himself from the subtle net that a false teacher weaves around his followers so that his ego may feed on them. When the aspirant meets a real Zadek, it will often only become apparent when his questions are answered, for the real Zadek will offer nothing, unless he is specifically asked. This is quite different from the fabulous promises made by the false, self-deceived or power-seeking teacher. Indeed the genuine Zadek will try to put the aspirant off, make obstacles and go out of his way to be difficult to contact. This in Kabbalah is a method by which the merely curious are quickly bored. Only those with a discerning eye will perceive the reason for the barrier, and to cross this may mean they have to sacrifice much time and energy in order to gain a small but vital piece of information. Real knowledge does not come from books, although a faint outline may be perceived behind the words. Only personal contact with a living connection makes it possible for Kabbalah to be transmitted, and even then one must be at least in a state of being prepared to receive. A man who thinks he knows may be quite deaf to an apparently casual but pertinent remark that can cause a profound change in another man. A rabbi can be perhaps more learned than a civil servant, but the latter might well be his Kabbalistic maggid.

When a man meets the teacher intended for him the work begins. Initially it is often an extended dialogue, stretching over many years, which touches on the serious side of life. Slowly there grows a relationship where the seeker at first guesses, then suspects that his acquaintance knows something he does not, that his conversation is based on a frame of reference that is not to be found in the ordinary world. Everyone has opinions, but in this case there is always an objectivity, a factor of scale, of depth, of balance that is uncommon because it also always relates to the state and potentiality of Man. One day when the aspirant is ready, the basis of this objectivity emerges. In the Kabbalistic Tradition, it is the Tree of Life diagram. It contains, the Zadek might or might not say, all the laws of the Manifest Universe. The seeker who has heard such claims before is often initially sceptical, but listens, because he is required to believe nothing until he has tested it for himself. Kabbalah is not a Way of belief, but of Knowledge. Because of this the first thing that has to be learned is its particular language. If the seeker is willing to forgo his preconditioned ego-Foundation and have an open mind, he passes his first Yesodic initiation and moves on to the Hod stage. The Zadek, if he accepts him as a pupil, then takes up the role as the man's temporary Tiferet or Guide on the journey back up the Lightning Flash to the Source of his being.

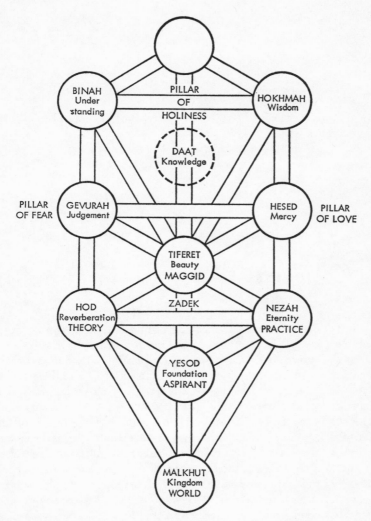

Figure 14. Aspirant. *In this Tree is shown the relationship between the aspirant coming up from the World of Malkhut and his maggid or spiritual teacher. Between them is the connection of the Zadek or honest man. On either side are the Ways of Fear and Love of God while in the centre lies the pillar of Holiness – the Way of Knowledge.*

11
Kabbalah

It is said that no one should study Kabbalah until he is forty years old. This is one of the many misleading myths that have grown up about the subject over the centuries. While this writer is over forty there are, and have been many younger Kabbalists. One of the greatest, Rabbi Isaac Luria, died before he was forty, having studied Kabbalah since his youth; and in the Western esoteric tradition Johannes Reuchlin, a perceptive Christian scholar, published the first book on Kabbalah by a non-Jew at thirty-nine, in 1494. Both lived at the end of a very creative period in Kabbalah that had begun at least five centuries before. During this time the form of the Teaching had been changed radically to adapt to the scholastic approach in religion and philosophy.

The impact on the traditional Jewish outlook was enormous, and there was considerable resistance from the orthodox, who wished to retain the strictly Hebrew character of their religion; and here develops a recurring phenomenon that was to plague Kabbalists down the ages. An example will illustrate. The works of Maimonides, one of the great rabbis of the Middle Ages, were banned at one time because his Aristotelian approach to religion was considered un-Jewish; indeed, his books were burnt as heretical. Today, however, he represents the epitome of the conservative view, his Thirteen Principles of Faith being a major institution in the Hebrew prayer-book. Such is human nature that what is old and tried must be the genuine article and what is new must be alien and false. It is ironical to consider that the traditionalists who condemned Maimonides probably never realized that the word 'synagogue' was Greek, and that many time-honoured customs in liturgy and domestic practice were of Babylonian and even Egyptian origin.

Kabbalah has always been a continuous process, that is, while its principles and aim are identical in every age, its outer form periodically changes as its language is modified to speak to the current generation. Thus we have Ibn Gabirol writing in Arabic in Moorish Spain and the Hasidic Rabbi Yitzhak Epstein using Yiddish, the Jewish vernacular of eighteenth-century eastern Europe, to explain a Kabbalistic point with greater clarity.

Kabbalah is still a living tradition, and it does not take its authority from one school, one body of literature or one person. There is the main Jewish line of Kabbalah that continues to hold and preserve the religiously acceptable format, but there are many others, both inside and outside the Judaic field, for Kabbalah has passed into Western civilization at several points. The first was through one of the greatest Kabbalists, Joshua ben Miriam, better known as Jesus, son of Mary, whose teaching is permeated with its terms and precepts. His Lord's Prayer when set on the Sefirotic Tree is a prime example, and it may be read from either end of the Tree's Lightning Flash with considerable illumination. The second input came from St Paul, who was trained by a major Kabbalist of his time, Rabbi Gamaliel, mentioned in the Acts of the Apostles. The third and later impulses into Western esotericism came in the Middle Ages and Renaissance, through scholars, intellectuals and mystics such as Pico della Mirandola, Reuchlin, Ruysbroeck and Fludd, not to mention several Jewish apostates, who projected Kabbalah into the European scene with such power that the intelligentsia of Christendom were for a while almost obsessed with the subject. Fortunately the fashionable aspect waned, and Kabbalah became only the interest of individuals and societies like the Rosicrucians who were devoted to helping people develop themselves spiritually. This of course is the prime aim of Kabbalah, and anyone who practises it in earnest is a Kabbalist, whether he be Gentile or Jew. The Teaching in any time, place or form is concerned with the whole of mankind.

Kabbalah can manifest itself in many ways. However, there are two broad streams both within and without every genuine line. One is the approach of Instruction, the other that of Revelation. These correspond with the two outer pillars of the Tree of Life, for not only is the Manifest Universe modelled on the Tree's basic sefirotic plan, but so are all lesser manifestations from the archangelic World of Creation down to the physical body of Man, and including the organization of a Tradition, which is a living organism in its own right. In Christianity, the Church is actually called the Body of Christ. In Kabbalah the same spiritual organism is named the Knesset or Assembly of Israel. Its door is at the Malkhut of Beriah, the realm of Pure Spirit. This Malkhut, the Kingdom, is to a Christian Kabbalist the 'Kingdom of Heaven' and to a Jewish Kabbalist the 'Gate of the House of Israel' or 'Heaven'.

If we examine the situation of our seeker who has just made contact with a Zadek, it will be seen that the Yeziratic Tree is primarily involved. In this Tree of the psyche, the mundane world is represented by the Yeziratic Malkhut, which is at the same time the Tiferet of Asiyyah. In physical terms it is the central nervous system of the body, the cellular basis of the brain and essence of the animal and vegetable level of existence. In Biblical terms we have seen it as Esau, the necessary natural part of even a spiritual man; for without some of the skills and desires of Esau even a saint would die. The seeker, outsider or aspirant stands in the position of Yesod, the ego-mind. This is his place of Knowledge in the World below, and his Foundation in the World above. Before he receives any training, all he has is his ordinary education and his life experience. These are flavoured with his body and ego types, so that he may be, for instance, a thinking extrovert or an introverted man of action. There are many combinations, depending on which triads are stronger or have been developed or retarded over the years.

When the aspirant meets a Zadek who may become his teacher or maggid, it is very important that his own type is correctly ascertained. To be merely considered a type is an affront to the ego, which always thinks itself rather special, but this is part of the Yesodic initiation, and no one can be accepted into Kabbalistic work until this test has been passed. It is a built-in fail-safe system that prevents the ego-orientated from gaining entrance into something for which they are not ready. When a man is prepared to accept that he is a type, he has already established some contact with his Tiferet, because he can at last see, if only for a moment, the Self's impartial view of the ego. This is the beginning of real individuality. The Zadek may have been waiting for this quantum jump for a long time, gently, slowly pointing the man's consciousness up the path of honesty by indicating the mechanicalness of ordinary living, the repetition of thoughts, feelings and action, and the limited range of the ego-mind. The maggid does this by applying his knowledge of types to illuminate, illustrate and demonstrate the man's bondage, in contrast to the moments of freedom which he enjoys while in a higher state of awareness. When the man recognizes the truth of what he has often been unobtrusively told, he realizes he must do something about it, and that the Zadek can help him. By accepting the need for a new Foundation he places himself at Yesod, directly below the Zadek, who takes up the role of Tiferet in the Tree that organizes the Kabbalistic Tradition. This alignment places both teacher and pupil, during the period of instruction, on the central pillar, by which, if it is willed from above, the Barakhah (the Blessing of Grace) may descend the middle column of consciousness. In this way the aspirant comes into direct touch with the Kabbalistic Tradition.

The two outer or functional pillars act as the approaches of Instruction and Revelation. Instruction comes down the side of Form, initially through theory in the sefirah Hod, while Revelation enters via Nezah on the side of Force. Both influxes meet in the mind of the aspirant at Yesod, to build the Foundation necessary to have a stable base in the next World. Traditionally there are several names to all three columns, each giving a different insight into their task. Sometimes the left-hand pillar is called the column of Justice, at others Severity. This indicates the method of strict discipline under Law. It is also called the approach of the Fear of God. The right-hand pillar is called Righteousness, or the approach of Piety and Love of God. Both these outer pillars have their positive and negative aspects, because excess in either causes imbalances that can create tolerance of evil on the one hand, and over-strictness on the other. A Zadek always holds the two approaches in equilibrium by concentrating on the central column of Clemency and Knowledge, the pillar of Holiness.

The role of the maggid in centring the aspirant in Tiferet and balancing the outer columns of Instruction and Revelation is essential; so much so that even those ecstatic mystics of Kabbalah who have no earthly teacher speak of an unseen discarnate maggid who watches over them. The seventeenth-century Christian Kabbalist Jacob Boehme, who for several days entered a state of cosmic and blissful consciousness in which he rose up Jacob's Ladder to view all Creation, had an unearthly maggid who told him that he would become another man:

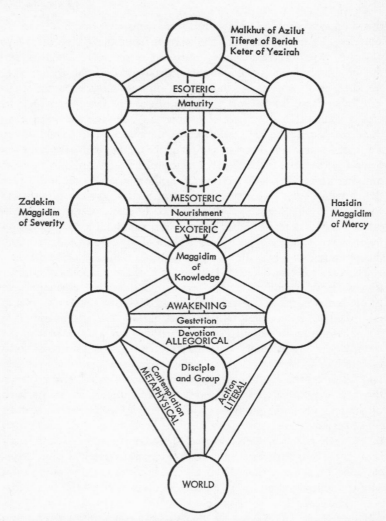

Malkhut of Azilut
Tiferet of Beriah
Keter of Yezirah

ESOTERIC
Maturity

MESOTERIC
Nourishment
EXOTERIC

Maggidim
of
Knowledge

AWAKENING
Gestation
Devotion
ALLEGORICAL

Disciple
and Group

Contemplation
METAPHYSICAL

Action
LITERAL

Zadekim
Maggidim
of Severity

Hasidin
Maggidim
of Mercy

WORLD

Figure 15. Seven Levels of Teaching: The Maggidim. *In this Tree of the Tradition are seen the three upper levels of evolved men who watch over and teach Mankind. They are sometimes called the Elders of Zion. To the left and right are the approaches of Justice and Righteousness while on the centre column is the Way of Holiness and Knowledge. Below are the three natural gates of entry to the Way. Gestation, Nourishment and Maturity describe the steps between Earth and Heaven.*

that is, a convert from the natural Jacob into the spiritual Israel. In Christian Kabbalah, this is 'is to be born again' or to 'become a new man'.

Unearthly maggidim are not uncommon in the history of Kabbalah. St Matthew is reputed to have written from an angel's dictation, and both Isaac Luria and Moses de Leon are said to have been taught by beings from upper Worlds. Rabbi Moses Luzzatto was imprudent enough to let it be known that he had written his works under direct, but discarnate, tuition and was persecuted by natural men for his association because they could not accept or understand the concept of an inner or upper World teacher. The existence of discarnate teachers was so taken for granted that one eighteenth-century rabbi remarked that in fact he preferred an incarnate one.

There are four approaches to Kabbalah, but seven levels of Knowledge. The first three, which are Literal, Allegorical and Metaphysical, relate directly to the three triads pivoted on Yesod. As such they are ego-orientated and are therefore in no way superior to each other. This is because although a man may know his Kabbalistic grounding in great detail through any or all of them, his level can be spiritually asleep, and therefore still located in the great Hod-Malkhut-Nezah triad of ordinary consciousness.

The fourth or Mystical level of Kabbalah begins with the shift into the triad Hod-Tiferet-Nezah, that of Awakening Consciousness. Here, above the threshold of Gestation, the Theory and Practice of the Teaching begins to become real to the aspiring Kabbalist. He is in touch, along the path of Honesty, with his Self, and he therefore starts to enter, as he glimpses the next World, the Triad of the Soul formed by Gevurah-Tiferet-Hesed. Here he comes into contact with the fifth level of the Teaching, and places himself, if they will accept him, under the tutelage of those in charge of the Exoteric or Outer part of the Inner Tradition. The people responsible for this level have many names, but two Kabbalistic ones will indicate their function. They are sometimes called the Zadekim, teachers of Severity, or the Hasidim, teachers of Mercy. They were known in the Middle Ages by the nicknames of the 'Terrors' and the 'Gentle' maggidim. Their method, like that of the schools of Hillel and Shammai in the Second Temple period, was to instruct, through Love and Fear, on matters concerning the Soul, and to encourage and correct the aspirant's knowledge of himself and all those events and people connected with his life and fate. This stage is known as the Work of Nourishment.

The next level is the Mesoteric or Middle part of the Inner body of the Teaching. Here in the great Binah-Tiferet-Hokhmah triad is taught the Instruction and Revelation concerning the workings of the World and Providence. This stage requires a cosmic level of experience and an objective consciousness. It is only for those who have established a real Foundation in the World of the Spirit: those who have truly entered the House of Israel, the Promised Land, the Isle of Saints, the Mystical Body of Christ, which is known by many other names in various traditions. This stage is known as Maturity.

The seventh level of Kabbalah lies above the state of Maturity. Its concern is with matters Divine, and not without reason, because of its direct connection with the Keter of Yezirah, which is also the Malkhut of Azilut, the Place of the Shekhinah or the Presence of God. This is the esoteric core and the heart of the Inner Circle of Mankind. It is said that here the Ten Elders of Zion are themselves instructed by the one fully developed Man, who acts as the Crown to all Humanity. Every living Tradition has this Chain of Teaching. Indeed there is reason to believe, that beyond a certain point up the ladder of instruction they are the same people. Whether they are Jewish, Christian or Moslem at this level is about as relevant as the question whether they are incarnate or discarnate.

For more ordinary mortals, the connection with a human, incarnate maggid is sufficient. Kabbalah is a long and gradual affair of growth. It cannot be hurried, nor played with. It is not for the immature nor for the foolish. To receive Kabbalah is to court change, and this is why, after the initial and real contact with a living Tradition is made, the aspirant's life often undergoes a dramatic transformation. Sometimes it manifests in the total break-up of an old situation and sometimes it triggers off a completely new and unsuspected possibility. When the Truth is touched upon, papered-over cracks are torn open, and things meant to be joined are fused in its light. Nothing can be the same after the Work of the Chariot has begun. As the Maggid of Nazareth said, 'No man having put his hand to the plough, and looking back, is fit for the Kingdom of God.'

12
Objective Knowledge

Over the ages and in many countries there have been several approaches to Kabbalah. In one place it was practised in pure Biblical terms, in another studied through cosmology, and in yet another via the science of numbers. Its form has been cast in ritual, prayer and contemplation, the evocation of angels and in the examination of the Hebrew alphabet, the nature of the soul and the destiny of Man. All these approaches are valid, provided they are aimed at bringing about the correct relationship between Man, the World and God. Anything less is mere scholarship or low magic.

Behind and governing the aim of Kabbalah is the Torah or the Teaching. In Judaism this is known as the Law. However it is not quite the Law that most Jews think of when they read the Scrolls of Moses on the sabbath. It has been said that the words of the Torah are like a fine garment, and that beneath the weave is the soul, and within that soul, the soul of the soul, which is God. While a natural man may be familiar with the scriptures to a remarkable degree it does not mean, as we have noted, that he perceives their inner content. He may obey all the Commandments scrupulously, and this is to his credit; but it does not mean he comprehends what the Law is really about. This requires a shift in view, a process of conversion that will enable him, not only to perceive the anatomy of the body and its workings, but to glimpse the soul within the body. This stage requires a preparation and training beyond the ordinary study of Biblical text and Talmudic commentary, which for all their learned skill and effort may take people no further than the literal stage of understanding.

There is a story the maggidim tell, which explains in allegory the relationship between the Kabbalist and the Torah or Teaching. The Torah is likened to a beautiful maiden who lives in a palace. The Kabbalist has heard of her beauty and continually passes by the magnificent building hoping to get a glimpse of her. One day he does so as a secret window opens and she looks out. It is no more than a glimpse, because she is heavily veiled. However it is sufficiently revealing of her Grace to make the Kabbalist fall in love with her. From that time on he is committed to courting her. He becomes totally devoted to his task, going to the palace at least once each day hoping that she will open her window again. In time she does, and if he is as attentive as he is full of ardour, she opens her window as if expecting him. Gradually they form a distant relationship, she making signs that indicate her interest in him. Eventually she beckons him to come closer to talk, although it is still through a veil. One day she removes the veil and he sees her face to face. They speak, and in the love that is present many secrets are given. Totally enamoured of her Truth and Beauty the Kabbalist wants nothing less than marriage, and when this is accomplished the lover and Beloved are united in One.

From the metaphysical view the Law is Objective Knowledge. It is the workings of Reality. Originating from the first World of Emanations it is eternal and unalterable. In every living spiritual tradition there is always a body of Objective Knowledge preserved by the Zadekim of that line. Kabbalah is no exception. The way it is presented, as noted, may vary widely according to time, place and individual needs. However while the format may be cast in the complex terms of the Book of Formation, in the story of the Exodus from Egypt, or in a simple ritual, its content is always the same objective truth about the laws that govern Man and the World and their connection to their Maker. In Kabbalah, perhaps the most famous formulation of these laws is the Ez Hayyim: the Tree of Life.

The Tree of Life is a diagrammatic scheme of the Sefirot or Divine Principles that govern Manifest Existence. It contains, and this is constantly repeated till learned, the concept of Unity and Duality, the idea of the creative trinity, the Four Worlds and the unfolding of the octave Lightning Flash between One and All, and back again. It also includes in its design the various minor laws of active and passive triads and the several levels of being on the central axis of consciousness. In short, it is a key to comprehending the laws of the World known and unknown to man. In the Tradition it is called the Key of Solomon, and not without reason.

The mere possession of Objective Knowledge does not mean comprehension. One may read the Bible over and over, have the Tree of Life on the wall of one's room for thirty years, and still understand nothing. Men have studied both formulations, taught and written books on Objective Knowledge, and still have missed the vital point that has denied them access to its meaning. This point is the desire to change, to convert. Many a remarkably clever person has failed where the more naive have succeeded, because they were reluctant to give up their old Foundation. As one Kabbalist said, 'It is hard for a rich man to enter the Kingdom of Heaven'. One must sell all one has, and this is very difficult if a man has invested a lot of time and effort on spiritual as well as material possessions.

The ability to change is the prerequisite of Kabbalah. To continue without being ready to change can precipitate disaster. Once the work is begun the laws of the upper Worlds alter the view of the aspirant, and if he wishes to go back, or hang on to his natural state, he may, like the wife of Lot who looked back at her old life, be turned into a pillar of salt. This is a symbol of a crystallized state, a psychology that is in neither heaven nor earth. It is a painful situation, for pure salt, while being a substance necessary for life, is too sharp if excessively present. Such people often wander between two Worlds with a contempt for the lower and a fear and anger at the higher for having been shown too much. This is the working of the laws of two Worlds, but out of harmony in a person who cannot make up his mind which set to obey. It is also an example of the Kabbalistic view of the Commandment 'Thou shalt not commit adultery', that is mixing things that do not belong to each other. Repentance, the other meaning of the word Teshuvah or conversion, is the solution to this problem; but often personal vanity is the barrier. The Commandment 'Thou shalt have no other gods before me' is not just a law designed for a people who had just emerged from an idolatrous country, but a statement of Objective Knowledge for use at all levels. The excessive belief in one's own importance is ego worship. And while ego is the functional identity and centre of a natural man's world, it cannot remain so in the prospective Kabbalist. He has to give up his ego's will for a brief time and submit to the instruction of his maggid in order to prepare to lay a new Foundation so that he may enter the next World safely. This is objective law. Any illegal entry, such as that through drugs, results in a fall, as many day-trippers into Yezirah have found. To obey law is also to acquire its aid. The bird in flying not only respects the laws of aerodynamics but uses them to its advantage. This knowledge, although acquired over many generations, has to be learned by each individual creature. So it is with the Kabbalist. The principles are inherent in every man and the universe about him, but to be able to rise up into the upper Worlds requires a great individual effort. This effort, under the instruction of the maggid, is directed towards the preparation for change by applying theory to practice.

To study the Dynamics of the Tree is not enough. A man may know all the theory of the pillars and triads, even be acquainted with the titles of the angelic hosts and the Divine Names of God, but if he has no idea where his own feet are he is useless as a Kabbalist. The beginning of the apprentice's training is to see his own true position; to observe while learning his metaphysics that he is for the most part confined to the lower face of Yezirah in the realm of mental mechanics. this is achieved by his observation and application of the objective laws he can comprehend so that he may gain some inkling of the same processes in the various faces higher up the Ladder of the Extended Tree. To help him, his maggid not only supplies the theoretical Hod information, but the active input of Nezah through exercises. These may consist of simple tasks of remembering the diagram of the Tree at certain times of the day, repeating a prayer, or performing the ritual of standing with his arms raised first thing in the morning and last thing at night, so that he physically senses the Tree through his body. Such exercises are designed to fix Objective Knowledge into the aspirant's Foundation by working down the paths from Hod and Nezah and into Yesod. This triad, called 'To go round in a circle', eventually transfers the knowledge from the non-luminous mirror of Yesod up into the triad Hod-Tiferet-Nezah, called 'To lock in position'. Here, having crossed the liminal line of ordinary consciousness, it is seen in the luminous mirror of the Self where the level of the aspirant is raised up the vertical path of honesty between Yesod and Tiferet. Such a process is slow, and is part of a major programme of preparation and change.

One of the features of transformation to be made during the probationary period, because a man only becomes a Kabbalist when he has a real connection with Tiferet, is the balancing out of the lower face. In his natural state the aspirant is a particular natural type, with a propensity towards one of the triads of thinking, feeling and doing, with the overlay of introvert or extrovert. The imbalance in his mental mechanics is worked on by the maggid, because if it is crystallized into the new Foundation it can cause a lot of trouble and be very painful to correct later. For example if a man is a thinking introvert he can be permanently over-balanced on the pillar of Form and become rather withdrawn and rigid, lacking the power to initiate and contribute beyond applying severe discipline. This phenomenon is not uncommon in all spiritual paths and indicates an undeveloped pillar of Force of Mercy. On the other hand, if a man is too much on the pillar of Force he can be excessive in his piety and lacking in discrimination, control and understanding. The well-intentioned religious fanatic demonstrates this clearly. As will be perceived, it is vitally important to bring harmony into the lower face of the psyche before the full powers of the Upper Worlds are allowed to descend, otherwise the man will not only be out of balance in himself but a menace to everyone else. This process is sometimes called purification.

The method by which balance is obtained is by working on the weaknesses of the aspirant; the thinker is made to do and feel, the feeler to think and do, and the doer to think and feel. In one case a thinking man may be placed in a situation where his mind is useless, and he has to depend on his practical skills. In another, the doer may be called on to act as a go-between in a circumstance highly charged with feeling, while a feeler is given a task requiring cool calculation concerning a purely physical problem, such as designing a small structure. All these exercises are carefully applied by the maggid, who may or may not explain his reasoning. However, in all cases he will require a high level of observation and often a written report from the aspirant. This is to cultivate the middle pillar of consciousness, without which all the work is useless. Many people reach the level of Hod and Nezah and never attain Tiferet. Without this degree of Self-consciousness they can never become Kabbalists, no matter how much information they acquire or the number of exercises they practise.

To be a Kabbalist means to be able, consciously and at will, to raise one level at least from Yesod to Tiferet. One may draw on the Form of the Left Pillar or on the Force of the Right pillar but if there is no life in the central column Grace cannot descend, and without Grace it is better to leave Kabbalah alone. A man may be powerful, but not necessarily good or useful.

Another part of the initial training is to build up a vocabulary about Objective Knowledge. This means the creation of a new and special language so that the aspirant and maggid know precisely what is being spoken of. This phenomenon is easily observed in many Kabbalistic documents, which are often unintelligible even to a reader familiar with their cultural and vernacular flavours. For, besides the bias of literal, allegorical or metaphysical presentation each text uses the terminology of its own particular school, which usually takes on the expressions of the maggid in charge of it. Such differences of language often explain apparent disagreements between Kabbalistic schools on, for instance, the various uses of different names for the soul or different uses of the same name. Thus the term 'Neshamah' is used as the highest soul by some and as the individual soul by others. In this book it is used for the latter and the word 'Ruah' or 'Spirit' is applied to the higher.

The use of a special language is twofold. Firstly, it enables the aspirant to approach Objective Knowledge without any preconceived ideas, and secondly, he may talk without difficulty to any other student of Kabbalah, trained by, or connected with, his maggid. This opens out new possibilities.

On the first point the non-Hebrew-speaking aspirant has a curious and distinct advantage over the Hebrew speaker because he can, for instance, invest the sefirot with meaning directly from his own experience, whereas the person of Jewish education has the drawback of not seeing the sefirotic names as basic principles, because they are already loaded with associations. This of course works both ways with a cultural heritage, but in the end it is of little importance, because eventually both have to construct a totally new way of looking at the World and themselves.

The second point, that of meeting others involved in the Work of the Chariot, refers to the stage where the aspirant is admitted, by invitation, to a group. This may take a long time to obtain, and it is entirely dependent on the efforts of the aspirant. Some people gain access almost immediately after their contact with the Tradition, others only after years. The move from the single connection of the maggid to working within a study group is an acknowledgement that the aspirant has the theoretical and practical basis of a Foundation. He knows and has experienced enough to see everything about that which is within him in terms of the Sefirotic Tree. He recognizes when he is working from one side of the Tree or the other, and can correct imbalances in the lower face, and at least admit that he lives in a state of bondage for most of the time. Perhaps the greatest qualification is that he seriously desires to raise his level up to Tiferet. Any other ambition takes second place, although legitimate achievement in ordinary life is not precluded. Indeed to remain in Asiyyah and yet be connected with the Worlds above so that their influx descends directly into mundane existence will be the next stage in his training. For if Keter does not reach Malkhut in the man he will never be a Kabbalist.

13
Groups

There are traces of working groups throughout the history of Kabbalah. They run parallel to the orthodox study schools and general religious life of their times, but do not always operate openly. Not taking into account the mythological line of mystical schools beginning with the angels instructing Adam, who passed the Teaching on through a human chain until the end of the Old Testament period, one of the earliest indications of non-Biblical Kabbalistic groups is in the two rabbinical schools of Shammai and Hillel (c. 30 B.C.), who were probably among the first to formulate the oral Tradition. Here began the written Talmudic commentaries on the Bible, vast texts in which esoteric teachings are scattered thinly. These fragments indicate the presence of an objective system, but such knowledge, it was said, could only be imparted fully in private to selected disciples, as the Hokhmah Nistarah – the Hidden Wisdom.

From the character of the two rabbis Shammai and Hillel can be deduced their Kabbalistic methods of working. Hillel was renowned for his mercy and Shammai for his severity. Between their two pillars they perhaps helped a whole generation of people to free themselves. Alas, as often happens, those who came after tried to perpetuate the system without really comprehending the methods, and by the time of Christ the two schools had become rivals. Here is an example of an organizational Tree without the middle pillar of consciousness to bring about a rise in level. Eventually both institutions sank to the polemics of political struggle, and only the Hillelites survived the destruction of the Jewish state by the Romans. Gamaliel, the grandson of Hillel, was the teacher of Saul of Tarsus, who later as St Paul taught basic Kabbalistic doctrine. Consider his remarks on 'children of the flesh' and 'children of the promise' (Romans 9:8), or his teaching on the body, soul and spirit.

Perhaps the most famous esoteric group, besides that of Joshua ben Miriam of Nazareth and his twelve disciples, was that of Rabbi Simeon ben Yohai who lived in Palestine during the second century A.D. The discussions reported in the Zohar commentaries illustrate well the special language used between members of a group, especially in the conversations on the Sefirotic Tree. Here the symbolism of a human form is used to describe allegorically and define the interaction of the Divine Attributes. Whether these talks actually took place in Palestine or in the mind of Moses de Leon, a writer in thirteenth-century Spain, does not matter. (We leave the real authorship of the Zohar for scholars to decide.) What is important is that it is an insight into a group at work. Such meetings obviously went on throughout the post-Temple period among the Babylonian and other dispersed communities. The Sefer Yezirah or Book of Formation is of this period, and so are the accounts that have come down to us of the ascent of Merkabah riders up Jacob's Ladder into the Heikhalot or Heavenly Palaces, the best known being the Book of Enoch.

As described in the short history of Kabbalah at the beginning of this book, the Teaching came from Asia to Europe probably before the tenth century; here it took root and generated the schools of Provence and Spain. From the writings, for instance, of the Kabbalists living in Gerona, we know that group work was one of the chief methods of study and practice. The volume of literature produced during this period also indicates that the aspect of secrecy was discarded, at least on the theoretical side. This indicates a need not only to counterbalance the attraction of the scholastic approach then prevalent, but to meet the requirement of a generation for whom the old orthodox answers were no longer convincing. This is the situation we face today; hence the current interest in mysticism and one of the many reasons for new books on Kabbalah.

The school of Isaac Luria during the sixteenth century was one of several study groups in the town of Sefad just north of the Sea of Galilee. Here Kabbalists met and worked with great intensity, forming companies that resembled the Essene esoteric communities of Second Temple times. Out of this period came the impulse that was to create Kabbalistic groups as far away as Poland. Indeed so powerful were the ideas propagated that the major disturbances precipitated in the stability of Jewish religious life caused an orthodox reaction against Kabbalah, and it was banned to the mass of ordinary people. The proclamation of Brody in 1772 still carries its weight to this day, and is one of the reasons why most Western Jews know nothing of Kabbalah. However, to the Establishment's credit, study for mature individuals was still permitted, and one comes across scrolls and books containing Kabbalistic tracts and diagrams published in my own grandfather's time.

In the mainstream of Jewish Kabbalah both the Sephardi and Ashkenazi, or the Oriental and European lines, continue. Various groups, some open and some closed, are to be found all over the world. Of these, some are working in the orthodox way and others, following a well-established Kabbalistic practice, are reformulating the Teaching into modern idiom so as to speak to the present generation. This creates, as has always happened, resistance from the religiously conservative, but Kabbalah is concerned with something larger than historic custom. It will respect tradition, if it still has content, and discard it if it does not carry the spirit. Cultural habits for their own sake put men in bondage, and the task of Kabbalah is to free those who want to be free.

On the matter of open and closed groups, it is a question of different levels and functions. The open are the outer aspect of Kabbalah. They may be merely repeating old material without understanding, as in some cases where Zoharic texts are treated like prayers to be merely recited; or they may be studying with the hope of gaining some insight. There are open schools whose object it is to expose some of the Kabbalistic theory or practice to those who might be interested. These operations are usually run by an inner group or a maggid whose object is to attract the attention of seekers and help them to find a way out of Egypt. The methods employed vary widely from metaphysical discussion through silent meditation to singing and dancing, depending on which type the school wishes to draw in. There are, as said, many pseudo-Kabbalistic groups and teachers, as well as schools that merely keep the memory, but not the spirit, of the teaching of long-deceased masters. The test is the quality of vitality and insight of the people involved. As one maggid said, 'If the approach does not make the practitioner joyous, then it is useless.' One can be happy as well as serious. 'By their fruits ye shall know them,' said another maggid.

Of the closed groups little can be said, because by their very nature they leave no direct trace. There are, as we have seen, some records, but these by definition change from the Oral into the Written Tradition and therefore only pass as faint after-images, since they are accounts of events that could never fully be described to anyone not present. The best one can do, in a book such as this, is to outline the principles involved and some of the practices; to attempt anything further would be to mislead and to promise something that even the great Kabbalist poets, such as Solomon Ibn Gabirol, find difficult to express.

D

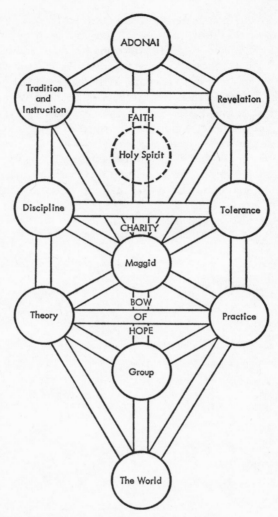

Figure 16. Kabbalah. *The Tree of approach to the Way is set out here. Below is the group and its relationship to the Teaching, while above in the intermediary triad, are the requirements needed to enter the upper face or inner aspect of Kabbalah. Hope, Charity and Faith define all the states necessary for direct contact with the yeziratic Keter of ADONAI – the LORD.*

14
Group Structure

The word 'cabal' has come to mean, in many European languages, a secret meeting; and there is some truth in this. Historically the reasons are twofold. The first is that sometimes Kabbalists were regarded as suspect heretics by their own people as well as by the religious rulers of the country they resided in. The second reason has been explained in the progression of the aspirant from the lower or outer world into the upper or inner where he can meet with others who have gained access to the lower Garden of Eden. Prior to this stage of development the person would have understood little or nothing of the language or objectives of the group, because he had no real Foundation in the World where they work. Another reason for such groups' hidden nature is that nothing can be given to the unprepared or, more important, to the half-prepared. While a son of Esau would merely be bored by the proceedings of such a group, an untrained child of Israel might overreact either way before he was ready to receive such knowledge. Therefore, only when he has sufficient theory and practice, experience and stability to enable him to work with a definite objective, is he invited to enter such a group.

The composition of what must be still a preparatory group varies widely although it follows general principles. In former times, in the mainstream Judaic line, groups were usually made up entirely of men, and most of these were, if not rabbis, very learned in Biblical study. This qualification was commonplace up till quite recently, because most Jews were taught the Bible and its Talmudic commentaries from a very early age and were steeped in its language and symbolism. Indeed one cannot enter an orthodox Kabbalistic school without such a background, because the study and practice methods are based almost entirely on the Zoharic commentaries on the scriptures. However Kabbalah is older and wider than even the Zohar, which many mistakenly regard as the ultimate authority. There is in fact only one ultimate authority in Kabbalah, and that is not to be found in books, groups, maggidim or even the hidden Zadekim. It is in the relationship between the Self and God.

Outside the orthodox Tradition is that line of Kabbalah which lies roughly halfway between the Church and the Synagogue in the European West and consists, usually, of committed Christians, Jews and religious non-conformists who seek spiritual growth, but have not found it in orthodoxy. Such a Kabbalistic line has assumed many garbs and names, and recurs throughout history, often only as a trace in a book, a social idea, in the arts, and even in government reform. Unlike many of the orthodox lines it brings men and women together in common groups. This is because most of the people involved are not living in religious communities, where segregation of the sexes is the norm, but under common life circumstances. Indeed one such group in the Middle Ages was called the Brothers and Sisters of the Common Life. A firm footing in mundane reality is a prerequisite for the Kabbalist, and particularly in his or her relationship with the opposite sex, which represents the complementary pillar in the group, in private life, and in the masculine and femine aspects of oneself.

In Biblical knowledge most Western laymen, be they Jew or Gentile, have a fair basic grounding from their early education. For instance, almost anyone living in a culture derived from Europe knows of Adam and Eve and if pressed remembers a surprising amount about the stories and characters in the Bible. And no one, even if he is totally ignorant of the scriptures, is without the archetypal figures of the Great Mother and Father of the unconscious, the Anima and Animus, so that whoever comes into Kabbalistic work is not entirely psychologically unequipped. The level of intent, experience and a common special language soon makes the aspirant a contributing member to a group.

Groups working in the unorthodox line of Kabbalah are composed of men and women. A quorum or minimum of ten is traditional, so that a complete sefirotic component is present. Ideally an equal number of each sex creates a balance, at the centre of which is the maggid, or the person who has been placed in the role of the teacher, because in relation to the others he is the Zaken or Elder. This title dates back to Moses, who instructed the seventy elders in the Sinai desert and appointed them as his assistants to teach the Children of Israel the Law. In time they became institutionalized into the Sanhedrin. The office of Presbyter performs the same role in the Church. In the case of a group the Zaken may have been given the job in order not only to impart what he has received, a basic Kabbalistic rule, but also to experience, through his Yeziratic Daat, the Knowledge that flows down from the Beriatic Yesod and through him while he is in the teaching role. There are several degrees of Zaken, but at this point it is sufficient to say that two distinct levels are required in group work, so that the influx of the upper Worlds is aided by the difference in potential between the upper role of the Zaken at Tiferet and the lower one of the group at Yesod.

A group is thus run according to the principles of the Tree of Life. On the one hand we have the left and right pillar of the sexes in the active and receptive functions, and on the other, the above and below of the upper and lower faces of Yezirah, with the maggid or Zaken in the centre of Tiferet. If we place the outside world at Malkhut, the group at Yesod and the theory and practice at Hod and Nezah we have what could be a normal social gathering. However with the maggid at Tiferet, the Triad of Hope comes into being. This configuration is sometimes called the 'Bow of Hope' in that it points the arrow of consciousness up the central pillar from Malkhut to Keter. The arrow is held by the group and the bow by the maggid, and in the tension generated by the pillars of Force and Form the arrow is shot into the upper Worlds. Its range is determined by the effort of the group and its accuracy on, or off, the central pillar by how far towards Force or Form the aim was at the moment of penetration. At such moments the Ruah Hakodesh, the Holy Spirit, which resides in the Daat of the Yeziratic Tree, may descend to indicate with its Presence, a hit on the target of realization. Such moments are unforgettable.

If theory is at Hod and practice at Nezah, discrimination may be placed at Gevurah and tolerance at Hesed. These two attributes are vital in the life of a group, for it allows the aspirants to exercise Judgement without being critical and Mercy without being over-indulgent. This keeps the way open for Truth to manifest without being drowned by excessive enthusiasm or thwarted by restrictive pedantry. The pivot of the group Tree is the maggid, whose position at Tiferet focuses Gevurah and Hesed into the emotional triad known to some Kabbalists as Charity or Love. This triad between the upper and lower faces is the next stage of consciousness up from the Hod-Tiferet-Nezah triad of Hope, and represents in the group, as it does in a man, the level of the soul. Here is the degree of Self-awareness where many things about one's own nature and those of others can be seen, but with Love. The synthesis of Gevurah and Hesed, as expressed in Tiferet, is called Compassion. It is in this triad of Love that individuals in a group meet in an emotional communion and share in mutual trust their experience with each other. Such a situation comes about because of conditions above and beyond the familiarity of ordinary social gatherings. These special conditions are generated by the aim, knowledge, common language and degree of discipline and integrity required of and by each member of the group. For example, the need to master the ego may mean curbing its assertiveness in one person or prompting it to come forward in a case of excess modesty, although never so that it becomes overactive.

Discipline in the group is important. Without it the community Tree would crack, even collapse, thus destroying a finely balanced organism capable of receiving something no individual could obtain on his own without training. Discipline is expressed outwardly in such courtesies as giving full attention in complete silence to someone speaking or performing a practice. Inwardly it is maintained by being ever watchful, continuously remembering to observe from the Self and always speaking and acting in the light of Tiferet. The moment the contact with one's own Tiferet is lost, the connection with the group's Tiferet is gone, and nothing happens outside the current daydreams of the ego that circle round the mechanical Hod-Yesod-Nezah triad. When more than half the group is in this state the quality of the meeting drops and drags down the others until the maggid applies a shock to awaken the slumberers. This shock can mean pressure on the side column that the group is down on, to bring about a reaction in them from the complementary column. Being exceptionally severe, for instance, invariably produces a response of Mercy that swings the group into equilibrium again. In an ordinary situation this technique might be socially offensive, but under the discipline everyone knows there is an inner reason for such action and it is accepted as an event to be studied in the light of objective law and its application.

The role of the maggid here is a responsible one. As the group's Tiferet he has to receive from above and impart below, and continually correct the group's tendency to sway between rigid formality and over-energetic diffusion. Thus, while teaching and guiding in this manner, he also endeavours to raise the level of the group, shifting it out of the usual Hod-Nezah polarization up the path of honesty and out of the triad of Hope to Tiferet. If he himself is down in Yesod, and even maggidim are human, nothing can happen for all the talk and exercises. Therefore he has to be constantly remembering who and where he is, because he is the group's link between Heaven and Earth. As the communal luminous mirror he is always looking inward to receive and reflect what may come down from any of the upper paths that focus on Tiferet. In this way he acts as the sefirotic junction-box for the group, acted upon and acting from moment to moment in a highly complex and subtle situation. This Seat of Solomon is the anchor of the group, and anyone who is prepared to accept the responsibility can take it over. Indeed, this can be one of the exercises which a person can be given. Under such conditions the individual in the Seat becomes not only the focus of the lower face of the communal Tree, with the group in the passive role at Yesod, but the means of contact with the upper face of Yezirah. This puts him in direct touch with the Binah and Hokhmah of the Tradition, giving him instruction and revelation about matters far beyond his personal comprehension. Anyone who has experienced this position and its living connection knows without doubt how Kabbalists obtain their Knowledge.

Besides being the Tiferet of the group, the Seat of Solomon is the Malkhut of the next World. Here also is the place where Jacob becomes Israel. In this conversion the upper face of Yezirah transforms into the lower face of Beriah, the Creative realm of pure Spirit. For the group the maggid represents the point of contact with the House of Israel. The great triad Tiferet-Hokhmah-Binah is called Faith. Faith in Kabbalah means not belief but knowing, and this is borne out by the presence of the Yeziratic Daat in this triad of the Spirit. Tradition places the Archangel Gabriel here, and he is the guardian of the Yesod of Beriah. By teaching, the maggid, if he is not already there, begins to make a firm Foundation in Beriah. This is his next step up Jacob's Ladder, so that there is a continuous process of ascension from the newest aspirant to the group to the raising of the maggid permanently into the House of Israel.

In Biblical allegory, the maggid plays the role of Moses on the

Mount Sinai of Tiferet, while the Children of Israel wait below in Yesod, having crossed the Red Sea in order to come up out of the Land of Bondage. They wait below the mountain of Hod-Tiferet-Nezah to be led, while the maggid receives his instruction from the pillar of cloud or Spirit that descends through the upper face of Yezirah. At the crest of the Keter of Yezirah is the Malkhut of Azilut, which is called by the God-Name ADONAI – Lord. Here is direct contact with the Divine. In Exodus the Lord warns Moses not to let the Children of Israel come too far up the mountain 'lest He break forth upon them. So Moses went down unto the people, and spake unto them.' There was still much work to be done before they could actually enter the Promised Land.

15
Group Dynamics

By the time the aspirant is invited to a group he should know his theory. This may consist of a working knowledge of the Sefirotic Tree. With such a basis he can at least initially grasp some meaning of the exercises given and follow the conversation in the group. However there are things he will not be familiar with, because each group has its own distinct character and vernacular which he must learn. This phenomenon occurs even in the strictly orthodox line of Kabbalah, because people are people, and the particular combination of types in a group determines its character, despite its classical Hebrew background. No two groups are ever identical. One may take its point of departure in Binah and be philosophical, or purely traditional, while another may start from Hokhmah and work along an original line of development. Another group with a strong Hesedic element will be emotional and devout in approach, in contrast to a Gevurah-orientated group which puts great store by discipline and purity. Those which work principally off Hod and Nezah are obviously very much in the nature of preparatory groups, not having established a substantial Tiferet connection. They are still confined to the lower face where theory and practice have not yet become fully part of their Foundation. The as yet unresolved character of such groups reveals their level.

If the Tiferet of a group does not materialize because of, perhaps, too much emphasis on one pillar, not enough conscious effort, or lack of connection between its members, the group is usually dissolved by the maggid, if it has not already disintegrated. Still births are not unknown in Kabbalah. One rule is that if there are less than seven at a meeting there is no evocation of the Spirit and the gathering is informal; further, if there are less than seven over four successive meetings, the group is disbanded. Such a phenomenon may occur because, at best, that phase of the Work is complete, or at worst, not enough members see any point in continuing. In the case of the former a new group may be reconstituted out of several old, but now disbanded groups, or its members may join an already existing one which is usually working at a more integrated level. This cellular system of birth, fission, fusion and death indicates the living quality of the Tradition.

Any group that goes beyond its life-span soon begins to be fossilized into an institution. There are many examples of this phenomenon inside and outside Kabbalah. Although well intentioned, such schools often grow beyond their human range, and the individual ceases to be important. When this happens, the perpetuation of the institution becomes the prime aim, with serried ranks of members working to preserve a long-dead yesterday and an unreal tomorrow. In Kabbalah, only today can be lived, only Now can be existed in. If a group has no sense of the present, it is either dead or unborn, and its body is redundant. Here is one of the reasons why there is so little known of the Oral Tradition. It occurs in the moment. Its task done, it vanishes leaving only a faint trace like a ship passing through the waters of time.

When people leave a group and do not return, there are several rules. First it must be determined why they have left. In one person's case it may be because the group method did not suit his type. For instance, a thinking man has no place at the ritual meals of the Belz Hasidim where physical nimbleness and strength are required as well as devotion. Nor would a man who only wished to pray be comfortable in a school studying the complex metaphysics of Rabbi Luzzatto. These leavers must seek their own paths, and if they are intent, Providence will lead them, if they are not directed by their contact Zadek, to the appropriate maggid.

With people leaving Kabbalistic work rather than leaving the group, it is a different matter. The reason for the move is usually because they have reached an ego crisis and do not wish to penetrate any further up the path of honesty. The rationalization for leaving Kabbalah varies widely from a dislike of formal systems to personal antipathy to the group as a whole, or the maggid in particular. Whatever the ostensible reason, the cause is the ego's defence of the person's existing image of himself. When this image is threatened by the change that must come with Kabbalistic work, the ego will fight to preserve its own sovereignty. This will manifest in many ways until there is a downright rejection of everything Kabbalah stands for. The parting is usually covered by a lie, either directly to the maggid, or indirectly through some other member of the group, which breaks the connection of mutual confidence. This severs the link, through the Tiferet of the group (which is why the maggid is often singled out for attack), with the Triad of Charity, or the Soul of the group. After this break nothing can be done, and the rule is that no member of the group should approach the person, unless they are called upon by him. This is by no means a punishment but a psychological rule that no pressure must be applied by Judgement or Mercy on that person, because free choice is his prerogative. Alas, occasionally the principle is seen as the cutting off of a heretic. This can, by nature, never be the case with people who are working in the Triad of Charity. Reserved friendliness is the correct balance between Gevurah and Hesed. Then, if the person's ego crises is resolved positively, and he wants to return, the doors of the group are still open. No one must ever be denied his birthright.

There is another reason why an aspirant may leave a group, and that is when he is sent out by the maggid. This can be temporary, so that the aspirant can reflect, digest and make his own the substance of the Teaching. Occasionally a man becomes too dependent on his maggid, and while it is necessary for the maggid to act as the man's Tiferet for a period, it is not permissible for him to assume this role permanently. While in some branches of the Tradition attachment to the maggid is part of the devotional method, it is not really desirable beyond a certain point, because then the maggid stands in the Way between the man and God, and this is contrary to the Commandments against other gods and bowing down to images. People make a false god of whatever they are devoted to, be it money, status or even a man, however exalted he may be. While the maggid can be the initial link in the chain of connection between Heaven and Earth, he must step aside and allow the man to make his own. It may require him to break up a relationship in which the aspirant's identification with his teacher is either gradually or suddenly dissolved, depending on the circumstance. The first method is accomplished by sending him away, and the second by demonstrating to the aspirant that the maggid also is human. This is sometimes achieved by the maggid performing an outrageous action aimed at destroying the attached aspirant's image of his teacher. Thus the false god is shattered and the person has to begin to take the full responsibility of his life for himself.

The other reason for sending a man away is that he has attained some permanent connection with his own Tiferet. He is a true individual. Such a person may be of more use to Kabbalah by becoming a maggid in his own right. In this circumstance he has finished his probationary period and the maggid will give him his last instruction, as an aspirant, to go off and consider the initiation of becoming a Zadek. Such a commitment means assuming the responsibility for others as well as for himself. To become a Zadek is not only to join a long line of people stretching through the generations but to prepare to enter the company of Just Men, the hidden Inner Circle of Mankind. For this major decision one needs to be absolutely alone, without any sort of outside influence, because the inner angel and devil will be enough to cope with during this sojourn in the wilderness. The Bible stories of Moses and Christ at the beginning of their missions describe this crisis.

The composition of a group, besides being made up of men and women, is also of various jobs and social aspects. This gives a group a richness and scope, provided all pool their experiences as equals, for the common good. The fact that one person is in a profession, another in commerce and another is an artisan makes no difference during a meeting, because all ego is left outside the group, below in the bottom face of Asiyyah. It must be so, or there could be no meeting. Ego separates people, and the mask of personality and status even more so. The only distinction in a group is body type, true individuality and conscious level. The first two are inherent, although they are in the process of being balanced, and the latter varies continually, until there is a permanent remembering of the Self. This brings about the phenomenon, unusual in the outside world, where a housewife will explain with deep insight a psychological point to a professional psychiatrist whose mind is perhaps obscured by his formal training. The significance here is not only the clarity of the housewife's vision, but the psychiatrist's acceptance. If both are committed to Kabbalah nothing less than the truth will do. It will be remembered that Spinoza was a lens polisher and Boehme a bootmaker. Binah and Hokhmah may manifest through anyone.

The three body types are symbolized in the Bible as the three sons of Noah, Japheth, Shem and Ham: thinkers, feelers and doers. A predominance of one type obviously loads a group in one of the small triads in the great triangle of Hod–Malkhut–Nezah, so that its method is strongly influenced towards contemplation, devotion or action. However, there is also the major influence of the maggid himself, who, although always seeking a balance, has his own way of doing things. This is the natural part of his true individuality, which is an attribute of Tiferet. It is said in the Christian monastic Tradition that the life of a monastery takes on the qualities of its abbot, and so it is in Kabbalah, because by virtue of the Laws of Providence those people who are in sympathy with that particular way of working are attracted to that Zadek. Another Zadek using a different approach might never be noticed. Therefore the maggid gathers round him those to whom he is useful and who are, in turn, useful to him. While such an idea may seem unspiritual, it must be remembered that everything must be paid for in the Universe. Action is rewarded by reaction and compensation in energy and matter; so it is in spiritual work. Indeed, without input there is no return, and as one Kabbalist remarked, 'The more you put in the more you take out. It is only law.'

The aim of the maggid is almost the same as that of the aspirant. The difference is a matter of level. While the aspirant is working initially for his own development, and later, also contributing something more to the group than the subscription for the bread and wine, the maggid is working on yet another scale. This may be theoretically known by all the group, but until they become Zadekim themselves they can only guess at its implication in time and space. Over the centuries Zadekim have operated not only in terms of their particular generation but on the span of Mankind. The folk stories discussed earlier, such as that of Cinderella, are evidence of ideas planned to be projected all over the world and repeated throughout at least two millennia. A Zadek of our time has the same brief as those before, that is to pass the Teaching on in such a way that, even if the people he trains do not fully comprehend the objective, they still carry on the work in their own way, so as to prepare people in the next generation. It is remarkable to note that, despite its myriad variations and chequered history, Kabbalah demonstrates the transmission well, for the basic Teaching has not changed. To quote Joshua ben Miriam, 'Till heaven and earth pass, one jot or one tittle shall in no wise pass from the Law, till all be fulfilled.'

Thus it is that there are three levels of Kabbalistic Work: that of the

Individual, which may be set on the lower face of the Yeziratic Tree; that of the Group, which fits into the Triad of Charity; and that of the Work for Humanity, which is concerned with the upper face of Yezirah. This face, of course, is the lower face of Beriah and involves all Mankind, dead, living and as yet unborn. In one word: Adam.

16
Meeting

Unless Keter reaches Malkhut a Kabbalistic operation is incomplete. Therefore let us set the scene of our studies in Asiyyah, so that we may glimpse what a group is like in recognizable terms.

As the past is gone and the future not yet come, we shall take the present as our time. This tense is the one Kabbalah works in. In it is all that was and shall be. Emanating from the first Crown, Existence descends through the Eternal World of the sefirot and into the World of Beriah. Here Existence is created before it passes on down to be formed in Yezirah. Out of the Eternal, Created and Formed Worlds, Asiyyah comes into Existence as a London square, full of blossoming trees and fragrance. Thirty thousand years ago this place was a patch of tundra a few miles from a glacier. Two thousand years ago it was part of a forest just north of a Roman road. Two hundred years ago it was a potter's field, and now it is an elegant square of houses in a fashionable part of Town. The Eternal is still there, Creation continues and the Forms are ever changing, as matter and energy, only for a moment, crystallize into the scene as we see it at eight o'clock on a particular spring evening at twilight. By half past eight it will be different, and in a thousand years' time quite unrecognizable, as the whole of Relative

Existence changes, yet remains the same. However we are only concerned with Now, because it is all we have and all we need to work with in Kabbalah.

From various directions ten people converge on a house in the square, some having taken half a lifetime to get there. They greet each other as intimates, although they may never meet socially or professionally. Entering the room they take their places in the semicircle of chairs facing the diagram of the Sefirotic Tree hanging by the maggid's seat. After exhanging news they all become silent. Slowly stillness descends as each person begins to meditate. Gradually the world outside recedes and its mundane problems fade, as quite perceptibly the atmosphere in the room begins to be charged and focused. The maggid, at the point when everyone is present both in body and consciousness, then rises. Spreading out his arms to make a physical Tree of Life he speaks the Great Prayer of Shema, which begins with the word 'Hear!' Slowly he speaks the sefirotic names one by one as he comes down the Lightning Flash in an evocation. He then calls upon the angelic Worlds for aid, and petitions that the Holy Spirit may grace their company. He concludes the ritual with the lighting of two candles to represent the pillars of Mercy and Judgement. The central column is filled by the group.

After the opening ceremony the Work begins. This may start with questions and observations, with the answers always given in reference to the Tree diagram, which becomes the focus of attention during most of the proceedings. In this way everyone sees precisely which sefirot, triads, paths and pillars are involved.

One question, for example, put to the maggid, is about the nature of meditative prayer. How does it fit on the Tree? He points to Yesod. This is the ordinary level of consciousness. Here the ego mind holds the Name of God to be meditated upon. It is reverberated by Hod and repeated by Nezah. With the two functional columns working through Yesod and the attention directed upwards, the consciousness is lifted out of the Hod-Yesod-Nezah triad into the Hod-Tiferet-Nezah Triad of Hope. Here the attention is directed, while the Name is still being sounded below, yet higher so that the Triad of Charity is entered. If God wills it, the Great Triad of Faith will bring the influx of Grace into Tiferet, so that the Self suddenly rises up the central column of the path called 'Awe'. Here the meditator reaches the non-sefirah of Daat and dissolves, if only for an instant, his sense of separation. When he emerges, he may perhaps re-enter, or descend, to become aware of himself and his ego mind repeating and reverberating the Name of God.

After the questions, answers and observations given by other people on the subject in the light of their own experience and understanding of the Tree, the group moves on to the main subject of the evening, which is the Children of Israel in the Wilderness. The Biblical passages have been studied during the week and each person puts forward his own understanding from a Kabbalistic view, relating the events to the parallel state in spiritual growth. Slowly a picture begins to emerge, not based on someone else's thought, however profound, but on their own realization within the group. Gradually the symbol of the Exodus is unlocked. One by one, each person sees the powerful natural desire to go back to Egypt where at least the Israelites were safe. Forty years in the Wilderness is a daunting prospect, especially when the route does not lead directly to the Promised Land. They recognize the rebel Israelites in themselves, see the doubting and the division in the psyche between that which stands for and against the Lord. They perceive the meaning of the Golden Calf, and how, like the ego, it is made up of things brought out from Egypt, its gilded image the Yesodic god to whom everything is sacrificed. The melting down of the idol takes on a psychological meaning that is not lost on anyone.

At certain points in the evening each person receives something meant especially for him and his development. It may come from the maggid or one of the other members of the group in an idea or casual remark, or it may come from deep within himself. The various sefirot, triads, paths and pillars are brought into play, revealing, illuminating and connecting many things that lie behind what appears to be a simple event. One person realizes how she is thrown from one side pillar to the other when there is no consciousness present in Tiferet. Another suddenly sees how the Ten Commandments fit into the Tree, starting with 'No other gods' at Keter. Yet another, like the faltering Israelites, is shocked into the realization that he cannot only never go back, but that a whole generation of bad habits has to die off in the Wilderness. Only one of the original slave Israelites, Joshua, entered the land flowing with milk and honey, and that was because he was constant.

The evening moves through many phases. Sometimes it is light and at others heavy. It swings from pillar to pillar, and occasionally rises in level, so that the group comes out of many into one. The ebb and flow is very subtle. Its medium is Yezirah, the World of the psyche, and many currents at several levels run counter and together with one another. The maggid is always watchful, guiding and interpreting, applying Gevurah and Hesed, and supplying Hod and Nezah in fragments of information and practices. At one moment he is the active pole, in the next someone else is. The focus moves to and fro, occasionally pausing in a protracted silence, when everyone is reflective. At one point there is more than silence present. It is a stillness so deep that everyone knows something other than themselves is in the room. It has the quality of a great wind in a vastness that makes it awesome. And then, as instantly as it came, it is gone and time begins once more. After a pause someone breaks the silence with a question. Eternity vanishes. The question is answered, but everyone in the room, except one person who momentarily drifted off into a daydream, is aware that they have been visited by a Presence.

From this point on, the meeting begins to resolve the evening's work into a formulation that is added to the Foundation of each person being constructed in the Yesod of the next World. The maggid sums up, yet he also leaves certain ends untied so that no one concludes that that is the complete answer. He then poses the question arising out of the realization gained that night, on the nature of the ego, and projects it on to the Yesodic symbol of Joseph and his coat of many colours. This will be the next week's work. They are to study the relevant texts and relate the symbol to their personal observation of the structure and workings of their own Yesods. They must bring in examples of its performance, its talents and defects and consider the idea of Yesod as the brilliant servant.

With the brief set for the next week, the group falls into silence and takes up a seated meditation posture. Slowly outer and inner quiet pervades the room. Gently each person enters into the same place and rises consciously into the Triad of Charity. There is love in the room fusing them together with all the people in the generations before and after, who have been and will be part of this Work. There is present for a moment something else, deeper and higher, as if there were watchers from another World in the room. The awareness of them is only fleeting, but quite distinct. The maggid rises and lifting his arms speaks the names of the sefirot as he returns from Malkhut up the Tree to Keter. He repeats the words of the Shema: 'Hear, O Israel. The Lord is our God. The Lord is One.' The group is frozen in stillness as they realize that the formal part of the meeting is over.

For a long moment no one says anything. People relax from their meditation posture, but it is not until the maggid speaks and brings the Asiyyatic World to the attention by opening the bottle of wine, that the group begins to re-enter the realm of the personal. Conversation begins and reflection on and unwinding from the first part of the evening proceeds. The atmosphere changes, but it is still the same operation. The group rearranges itself into lesser units that talk about trivia as well as Kabbalah, yet it is never forgetful of why they are there. There are still questions and answers, statements and even disagreements. One person sees a phenomenon from one side of the Tree and another from the opposite pillar, with a third, not necessarily the maggid, bringing them into a harmony by placing the observation in context on the central column. The maggid questions each person on what he has learned that evening, so as to fix it in Yesod. He suggests an exercise to one person in order to help him study Hod and Nezah. Another brings up a problem, and this he deals with by making the person place the elements on the Tree; he then asks what solution the person would recommend in the light of the imbalance indicated between the sefirot. The man sees the point and is told to practise his own advice. Such conversations go on throughout the rest of the evening, with some realizations having yet deeper significance than when they first appeared during the formal session. By the time the evening reaches its natural conclusion, when the last person has departed after a private consultation with the maggid on a personal question, everyone will have moved and changed a little. Like the blossom-filled square on that particular night in May, nothing will ever be quite the same again, for the process is continuous, until the return to union with the ultimate One.

Such a Kabbalistic meeting is by no means typical, because every group is quite different in its maggid, members and method. The meeting described is a fictitious synthesis, as is the maggid and the place. However the events are not, and may be recognized in different forms over the ages and in widely separated places. We read, in the Zohar, of the Idra Zutta Kadishah or Lesser Holy Assembly meeting in the house of Rabbi Simeon ben Jochai. Here the Companions, as they were called, gathered to discuss Kabbalah even though Rabbi Simeon was dying. Indeed the detailed account of the dialogue concerning the Sefirotic Tree takes the meeting right up to the death of the maggid, when the Rabbi acting as the group secretary realized on looking up from his notes that his teacher was dead. A perhaps less a dramatic account of a Kabbalistic school's approach and methods is to be found in the writings of the Habad movement of the Hasidim in the eighteenth and nineteenth centuries. Here, in 'courts' as they were called, men like Rabbi Dobh Baer would teach Kabbalistic theory and practice. And this might not be always in an obvious form. As one aspirant remarked, 'I come to see how the maggid ties up his shoelaces.' There are as many ways to receive and impart Kabbalah as there are people.

17
Out of Egypt

What then is the situation for our Child of Israel, now that he is working in a group? First we must review the story so far.

To begin with he now recognizes the reality of the human condition. Most of mankind is in bondage and lives in the vegetable state of eating, sleeping and propagating. However, the condition is optional. No one is obliged to exist at this level. Everyone has the choice to leave Egypt, but they do not, because they prefer the security of the known and familiar however difficult and painful the life might be. Millions are born to grow, mate and die without more than an inkling of another form of existence. Such a realm is rigid, its laws governed by mechanical and organic rhythms, each day much like the next, except for the occasional dearth or glut created by events in an upper World. It is a plant-like existence, each generation a season's leaves on the Asiyyatic Tree. As such it has its place in the relative universe as the seed-bed of the soul, but a being, like a seed, can remain in the ground until the end of Time unfructified and undeveloped, so that on the Day of Jubilee it is replanted and remains unfulfilled for another Shemittah or Great Cosmic Cycle. This is an experience the Child of Israel does not wish to repeat.

On the next level is the Land of Edom ruled by the Sons of Esau, the animal man. These beings dominate the earth, their empires flourishing and fighting, and if not destroyed, decaying; to leave only the trace of a moment of vainglory. Such people have their place in the cosmic scheme goading or leading the mass of mankind into change. This, be it through the conflict or diplomacy of Force and Form, serves a purpose, if only to shake vegetable men from their slumber. In such periods of change, whether they are slow or sudden, the vast majority of humans have a glimpse of evolution and see that life can be more than the secure state of being rooted in a plant-like condition. Indeed, the kings of Edom are powerful; and yet they have no command over themselves. They possess a will; but it is governed by their desire, which is subject to mindless attraction and repulsion. They are entirely subject to the whims of their own animal nature, their lives ruled by the need to reach and maintain a dominant position. When physical vitality begins to wane, they are soon overthrown by younger kings and queens. There is nothing permanent in this natural domain, and so the seeker after Eternity looks for a way out of death into immortal life.

The beginning of the Way was not easy to find, although there are traces of it everywhere. The seeker read and heard of it, but he never found an actual door, until he met a Zadek, and even then he had to wait until the door was opened on to the first threshold. The entrance into the lower Garden of Eden came as a delightful surprise, especially the discovery that there were others who had also crossed the Red Sea. In the haven of the group a sense of reality not only brought him to conclude that he had not been as mad as the mundane world had thought him, but to the realization that a great deal more work had to be done before he could properly enter the estate of the Promised Land. The threshold was the period symbolized by the forty years in the Wilderness. Guided by the group's Moses, he and the others had now begun to breed a new generation of attitudes, while the old habits, born in Egypt, slowly died off. This was accomplished by the balance of study and practice. The work was hard, but manna fell every day from Heaven, sufficient nourishment for that stage during the journey through the desert. Each week on the sabbath they met below the Mount Sinai of Tiferet, from which the maggid instructed them on the Law. Sometimes the Cloud on the peak descended, and the Holy Spirit of the Shekhinah was close to them, but it always rose and went before them, leading them on as they prepared an inner tabernacle to to receive it permanently.

The preparation consisted of first recognizing that one had a physical body, that it was governed by laws, and that these laws, although manifest in a mineral and organic form, were the same in principle as those which brought Existence into being. Such a realization was important, because it placed the physical body in its proper context in Creation, and dealt with the tendency in some spiritual seekers to deny its place and purpose. In Kabbalah the body is never devalued, tormented or cut off from consideration in even the most exalted of experiences. It is the lowest face of Jacob's Ladder, therefore the one by which the Will of Heaven manifests itself on Earth. As pure materiality, it is without direct connection with the upper Worlds; and this is one of the chief reasons Man is present in incarnate form. Through Man and his conscious intention, the mineral, vegetable and animal Kingdoms are placed in a position to receive the Divine Influx. Outwardly this may be expressed in civilization and inwardly in the participation of the mineral, organic and vital levels present in Man's body and animal nature. This much the aspirant had learned and now began to practise.

On the Tree, Malkhut is called the Guph or body. On the extended Ladder of Worlds the Malkhut of Yezirah is the central nervous system, the Tiferet of Asiyyah. Yesod, the ego mind of the Yeziratic Tree of the psyche, is the focus of the many psychological facets or Children of Israel that go to make up the complex identity of the image we have of ourselves. Six hundred thousand Israelites came up out of Egypt. This number may be the scale of intellectual concepts, emotional complexes and physical habits that manifest through the ego, not to mention the selection of masks donned and taken off each moment by the personality. All these aspects of Yesod have to be identified and recognized as the reflection of events occurring elsewhere on the Tree. Moreover, it must be realized that the phenomena displayed on the screen of the ordinary mind may be conscious or unconscious. When they are unconscious, the state of realization is no more than mental mechanics.

The study and command of the Form and Force of the lower Yeziratic face is the first practical work to be carried out. This involves observation of the vegetable and animal levels present within a person. An exercise in the appreciation of the vegetable world is the practice of fasting. This abstention from all food and water for twenty-four hours is an ancient Kabbalistic technique that has degenerated into a penance. Its original object was to demonstrate the power of the vegetable processes of Life and our dependence on them. Without food the organism is depleted both of energy and of form. This means that the Hod and Nezah of the cells and organs do not function properly, which throws the autonomic system of the lower Asiyyatic face into an emergency status of drawing on its reserves. When the fast goes beyond a certain point, all the vegetable rhythms are put in disarray, and unpleasant sensations such as headaches occur, as the finely balanced metabolic set of the organism is disturbed. During the fast the aspirant is meant not only to note the phenomena of vegetable experience, but develop the capacity to observe objectively. This will require him to shift his level of consciousness up from the Daat or Knowledge of his body, and from the simultaneous ego Yesod, into the Self of Tiferet. If he can sustain this vantage-point often enough, he will observe the Daat-Yesod ego squirming under the pressure of the vegetable soul demanding attention. Indeed he will have to contend with the ego as it attempts to get him to eat something. He will observe its full capacity, from direct demand to the subtlest cunning. His success or failure also helps the aspirant to rate his level of will power, a vital prerequisite if he is to go any further in the Work. The fast is a good training exercise because it reveals many levels; however, it must not be abused. In Kabbalah a good physical state is the best for any operation; therefore, once the point of the task has been made, it is concluded. 'We must fast to live, not live to fast' is a good reversal of an esoteric maxim.

The study of the animal part of human nature brings out a basic Kabbalistic attitude: that one must relate to life. Kabbalah is no use to a person who wishes to withdraw from the world. While it is necessary to have periodic solitude for private ritual, prayer or contemplation, it is in the social and public domain that much of the Kabbalistic Work is done, although it is rarely seen. As an exercise in studying the animal level, an aspirant may be given the task of going out into the market-place and doing business. Here he will see all the characteristics of animal behaviour at work. Moreover, he must perform the task without being involved in the excitement, the gain and loss, and the pride of success. He must be indifferent yet skilful in attack and retreat. He must be able to smell the state of the market and observe the animal in himself preparing to fight or fly. He has to identify the subtlest forms of animal behaviour in himself and others, so that he learns to perceive what is truly human. Animals, for example, do not have conscience or compassion. They feel fiercely when working from Nezah and sensitively when operating from Hod. Observe the switch of a cat from the sleepy, affectionate pet by the fire to the ferocious and merciless hunter of fledglings. The prospective Kabbalist must know which triad he is in. He cannot afford to mistake vegetable well-being for Bliss, or animal elation for Ecstasy. He should be able to recognize and rise above these two organic states at will. His soul depends upon it.

In Kabbalah both the vegetable and animal souls are sometimes combined into what is called the Nefesh or Vital Soul. This natural entity is confined to Asiyyah, and therefore occupies the Asiyyatic part of the lower Yeziratic face. It is said to fill out the Zelem or image vessel of the incarnate being, which half belongs to the World of Formation. It has been called by some people the etheric body, which disintegrates at death, as the Trees of Yezirah and Asiyyah separate.

The Nefesh inhabits the upper face of Asiyyah. However in simultaneous existence are the mental mechanics of the lower face of Yezirah. These operate in the triads pivoted on the Yesodic ego. Here also is a field of operation in the aspirant's preparatory training. First he has to learn to identify the triads, observe how there are two that always make him look outward to the World of Asiyyah and two that cause him to reflect. Exercises to bring these pairs into prominence may be given to him. For example he may be told to learn all the root word meanings of the letters of the Hebrew alphabet. Here the logical triad of Hod-Yesod-Malkhut will scan, while Nezah-Yesod-Malkhut will continue to repeat the exercise until the letters and their associated ideas have been fixed in Yesod. At the same time the inner triads, based on the Yesod-Tiferet axis, will begin to reflect and react, as the scheme of the concepts embodied in the alphabet begins to crystallize. When the aspirant is told that a letter fits on each path of the Tree, one between every two sefirot, he will not be surprised to see where some of them are placed. For example, he may well have intuited that the letter Tsade, meaning 'honest' and 'just', applies to the path between Yesod and Tiferet. Nor might he be surprised to find that the letter Chet, meaning 'awe' and 'fence', is on the path from Tiferet to Keter.

These conclusions may come from the memory stored in the unconscious of the incident in Exodus, where Moses says to the Lord, 'The people cannot come up to Mount Sinai: for thou chargedst us, saying, set bounds [or fences] about the Mount and sanctify it', and the Lord says to Moses, 'Thou shalt come up, thou, and Aaron with thee: but let not the priests and the people break through to come up unto the Lord, lest he break forth upon them.' This text may not have been read for many years, but the facility of Hod, in conjunction with Tiferet through the conjoining path of the letter Ayin whose root means 'study', may fish out the recollection from a remote corner of memory to flash it on the screen of Yesod. The complementary triad of Tiferet-Nezah-Yesod would react strongly and lift the ordinary awareness of Yesod into Tiferet for a moment of self-consciousness. Such events are pieces of realization placed one by one into an ever-growing and deepening jigsaw of knowledge.

Perhaps the most important exercise is continually to reach up from Yesod to Tiferet. Such a connection is absolutely necessary in any of the practices used by Kabbalah. One may perform the most elaborate ritual, pray incessantly and contemplate the Sefirotic Tree for a life-time, but if there is not a real connection between Yesod and Tiferet it is all useless. One action, solitary prayer or single idea performed from the Self will bring the upper Worlds into communion. Without the centring of consciousness on this Heart of Hearts nothing can happen. Solomon's Seat is there, but it can only be made a full reality when consciousness has mounted up the path of the Zadek to take a permanent place in the being of a man. To attain this state requires will, patience, reliability and training.

This, then, is the situation in which our aspirant finds himself. He has crossed the Red Sea and can never go back, except as a slave or as a maggid in his own right.

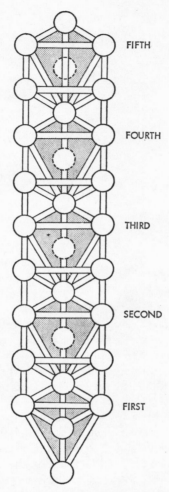

FIFTH

FOURTH

THIRD

SECOND

FIRST

Figure 17. Five Gardens. *The Five Gardens of Jacob's Ladder represent distinct stages in the four Worlds. All, except the highest and lowest, contain two simultaneous faces, one from the upper and one from a lower World which are converted, by the transformation of the lower Daat, into the higher Yesod. The central or Third garden is a special place because three earthly and three heavenly Worlds meet there.*

18
Preparation

Before an aspirant can be allowed to do any real Kabbalistic Work, he must be well grounded in his mundane life and in the theory and practice of Kabbalah: that is, he must be stable in Malkhut, Hod, Nezah and Yesod. Until he is truly reliable in these sefirot he cannot be a Kabbalist, for without this preparation he has no strong connection with his Tiferet. Even now, although he does rise up for a moment's glimpse into the World of Spirit, it still does not mean that he can do it at will, or sustain himself there at that level. Therefore he is still below, between Tiferet and Yesod in the psychological realm of awakening consciousness. As yet he is not on the Way proper, which begins at the Tiferet gate to the House of Israel.

'Many are called, but few are chosen,' said a Kabbalist. This is because only those people who are prepared to take on the full responsibility for their actions can be trusted to serve righteously. As said, a man who does not seriously consider the results of his actions is a menace not only to himself, but also to others. Therefore in Kabbalah, the aspirant is trained until he understands the Laws of cause and effect. This is accomplished over a long period and with many exercises, so that he does not initiate an action he is not prepared for, because it must be remembered that a willed impulse directed into the upper Worlds returns to its place of input. Such semi-magical operations are generally discouraged in Judaic Kabbalah. They are only permitted when there is no other course open, and then strictly under the fail-safe clause that the Lord wills it.

The methods of training in Kabbalah vary widely, but they all fall under the three main categories of literal, allegorical and metaphysical. These correspond to the physical, feeling and thinking aspects of man, described by the sub-triads of the Great Triad Malkhut-Hod-Nezah. They all focus on Yesod, so that gradually all three approaches will be absorbed into the new Foundation that is reforming the ego.

The result of this work is that the person often undergoes a change of personality that his old friends and family find difficult to recognize. Occasionally they become hostile to him, for he no longer plays their psychological games. Sometimes the transformation is so great that relationships of long standing are split and jobs with great promise or security are discarded. The early lives of many saints and Zadekim illustrate this well.

This is not the only problem encountered during the preparation period. There is also the temptation on the part of some aspirants' egos to claim the Kabbalah (or indeed any Tradition) as a personal possession. Here is the first test of the new Foundation. Such people think they are Kabbalists and play the Yesodic mystery role of knowing all about it, when all they have is a smattering of theory and one or two experiences of practice. Fortunately when really put to the test their knowledge is soon exposed in true shallowness and their image collapses. For some it may be no more than a passing phase of Yesodic euphoria that demonstrates the misuse of power; but for others, those with dishonest intent, it may prevent them from going any deeper into Kabbalah. There are many such people, both in the orthodox and unorthodox fields, who are frozen in growth by a Yesodic image of knowledge which is only a faint reflection of the living Knowledge of Daat.

Such temptations occur all the way through the preparatory stage. One may become too preoccupied with the information of Hod, or obsessed with just performing it in Nezah. Both need each other and can only work correctly when reconciled on the central column.

Besides these minor temptations there is the major one of Tiferet. This initiation, however, does not confront the aspirant until he becomes a real Kabbalist.

If one examines the extended Tree of Jacob's Ladder it will be seen that there are five Faces. These may, according to one tradition, be called the Five Gardens. Set out one below the other, they enclose the presence of two Worlds in each, except for the lowest and highest Gardens, which are purely Divine or totally Earthly. From above comes the Will of God, which descends as Manifest Existence and Grace. From the bottom or first Garden a man may ascend, entering greater and greater places of Beauty and Truth, until in the Fourth Garden he stands in awe before he enters the Fifth Garden of Unity. The stages we have been discussing so far have been the rising up out of the First into the Second Garden. This place is the natural home of the ego, where it studies, practises and prepares a man to enter into the Third Garden. The training at this level is a passive process of learning which has to be completed before Knowledge can be actively applied.

Preparation means to be able to receive and impart. The three exercises that follow are designed so that the degree of reception determines the quality of Knowledge given. The exchange is precise, and is paid for by the amount of conscious attention invested by the aspirant. Such exercises are a training for real Kabbalistic Work: before one can perform the acts of ritual, devotion and contemplation, one must learn how to hold and direct the attention in a complex situation. Where attention is, there is power. If it is focused unwaveringly on any part of the Sefirotic Tree, that level will operate directly through the Kabbalist. Such a responsible position is not taken lightly. To receive and impart requires great preparation.

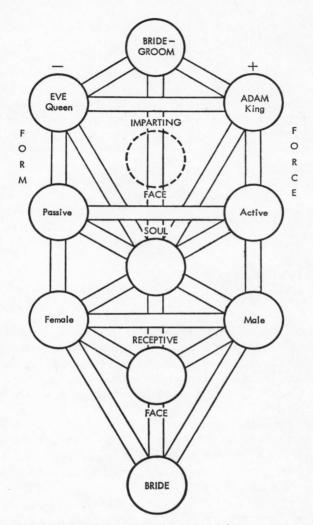

Figure 18. Male and Female. *Here the positive and negative aspects of the Tree are set out to illustrate how the literal phrase 'Male and female created He them' has many depths and meaning. The interrelation between the two poles is vital in the maintenance of the Universe, their conflicts, complements and unions giving power and structure to the beings, time and places contained therein. The central column is their area of communion.*

19
Literal

It is said in the Talmud that if one wishes to observe the invisible, then one must observe the visible. Therefore the first exercise is concerned with the literal and mundane, in the light of Kabbalah. Let us assume that the quotation 'male and female created He them' from Genesis 1 has been given to the aspirant by the maggid to be studied from a literal view.

Set on the Sefirotic Tree, the text refers to the great Father and Mother at the head of the side pillars. These perform as the active and passive principles that work all the way down through all the Worlds. Known sometimes as the King and Queen, they are more familiar in the shape of Adam and Eve.

Beginning at the literal level the aspirant's task is to observe the two interacting functional pillars in the most ordinary circumstance. Assuming he is a practical man, the first thing he will detect is the reciprocation of the active and passive principles at work in physical and mechanical processes. Thus he will perceive how all machines are based on the interaction of Force and Form. No petrol engine, for example, can work without the power of its fuel, the positive principle being confined by the limiting walls of the combustion chamber, the negative principle. If the highly explosive mixture were not constrained, its energy would be lost to the engine. Here the female cavity of the cylinder block contains the male burst of rapidly expanding gas and converts it into manipulative Form and Force, under the direction of the engineer, the representative of the third and middle pillar of consciousness. What the machine is or how complex it might be makes no difference, it still has to follow the law of positive and negative interaction. Consider a simple electric wire with energy flowing through its form, or a complicated rocket flying to the moon: both use the same active and passive principles.

The next thing that the literal aspirant might examine is the organic world. Here again he will find the male and female principles at work. Most plants, he will discover, contain a male and female aspect as manifest in the stigma and stamen. The former, as the female gynoecium, contains the ovules of a flower, while the latter produces the male-type pollen that will fertilize, if not the same plant, then another of the same species, so that reproduction may occur. This male–female axis runs throughout the plant kingdom and precipitates a most complex process involving interaction at many levels between the inorganic and organic realms. For the aspirant who is perhaps a scientist by profession, with high material criteria to work to, the Kabbalistic exercise brings no problems; he can see the Tree at work, if he knows how to look down the electron microscope, even to the frontier of that place where the Force and Form embodied in waves and particles, dissolve into absolute nothingness, the lower end of the Ladder of Jacob.

Even if the aspirant is not a scientist he can still study the manifestation of the male and female principle in the ordinary world about him. He would have observed ever since he was a child that the animal kingdom is divided into sexes, every creature belonging to one or the other. Such a division is so readily accepted that often its full significance is missed. With even a little experience with pets or farm animals, it is quickly learned that the males, on the whole, are stronger and more aggressive than the females, who tend to be quieter and slighter, except when they are with young. This difference in sexual temperament is quite marked and affects whole communities of animals, separating their social order into a constant polarization, be it the segregation of mature bull and cow elephants or the pairing of ducks over a lifetime. This potency of the tension and attraction between male and female generates a multiplicity of sub-phenomena ranging from the elaborate water dance of some fish, through the courtship display of the peacock,

E

and the building of nests and lairs, to the parental roles of apes. For the Kabbalist aspirant, here is a physically observable mine of information about the interaction of the two outer pillars of Force and Form.

When it comes to the examination of mankind it will be seen, by our practical investigator, that the human world contains both the vegetable and animal kingdoms in its biological make-up, and that human societies are subject to the same male–female polarization. Besides the obvious sexual differences there are a whole mass of social and economic divisions that define types of work, play and status. In some societies, for example, the difference actually keeps the sexes apart except for mating. In more sophisticated communities there is a mixing, but the dividing line is still present when it comes to courtship and often profession. The male–female battle is a familiar game in Western society; and, while it creates much material for the entertainment world, it is a fiercely played match in workplace and home. The medieval book of Courtly Love may be dated by its customs, but its precepts are based on the same forces that have been at work between male and female since the Stone Age. This, to the perceptive Kabbalist, particularly illustrates the phenomena of the two pillars at work in the great lower triad of Hod–Nezah–Malkhut, with Yesod at its centre. At this level there may not be much individual participation, because the people involved are more often than not caught up in an unconscious organic impulse to propagate the species rather than to relate as persons. Such a view is not a criticism but an impartial observation that the natural level of Mankind is not so much concerned with individuals as with maintaining or perfecting the species.

Moving from the purely biological into the bio-psychological aspect of the mundane world about him, the literal Kabbalist will see that society is permeated by the male–female factor. From a very early age children are taught directly and indirectly how to act as men and women. Boys copy their fathers and girls their mothers, be it in the workshop or kitchen, in private or public, or in crisis or calm. If a child has no obvious father or mother it will seek out a person and project the role upon them, so that the child can model itself upon the male or female adult.

In any society the male and female roles are preserved in social custom, not because they are a mere tradition, but because they are fundamental to the community. This stems from the male and female division in the collective unconscious as well as at the biological level. Evidence of the bio-social polarization is to be seen in the manner a community leans towards the matriarchal or patriarchal emphasis, depending on which outer pillar of the group's Tree is stressed. Further evidence of the projection of the inherent male–female presence is the parental role in which the leaders of a community are cast. Many communities have uncrowned kings and queens, despite their demo-cratic constitutions, because of the fundamental need for a great father or mother figure. This appeal is universal, because it is the collective unconscious response, at the social and political level, to the great archetypes of the Animus and Anima inherent in the body and psyche of humanity. In Biblical terms they are known as Adam and Eve.

The power of these two great archetypes within a community is considerable. It not only governs the relationship between the sexes in work and play, but the general balance and well-being of the society. At certain points in history the Animus can generate wars or periods of great creation, while emphasis on the Anima or female side will incline a people to a more conservative, peaceful but rigid epoch. All nations swing from male to female pillars and back again, and this is to be seen in their politics, arts and fashions. In times when the national Tree is well out of balance, and the active and passive roles in a community are scrambled, often much sexual and moral deviance occurs on the social level, as political extremists of revolution (active) and reaction (passive) rend the community. This happened to Germany between the two great wars. Thus a Kabbalist can, by surveying the newspapers, fashions and moods of a country, perceive the active and passive balance of its national Tree and so determine its stability and vitality.

On the more intimate level, the literal approach can take the observer out of the social and into the purely psychological field. While going about his mundane tasks and pleasures the aspirant learns to identify active and passive roles taken up by people. Some he will see switch from one to the other, such as becoming the female while listening and the male while talking. Some people, irrespective of sex, continually take up one pillar: one man may be a reflective thinker, another may adopt an ever-accommodating state of passivity or fussi-ness that makes his colleagues regard him as an 'old woman'. On the other hand it might be a high-powered girl who generates too much stimulus wherever she goes, while another woman operates actively with controlled efficiency. These different roles are often crystallized on to one column in most people, as the aspirant will discover when his maggid draws his attention to his own fixed habits and psychological postures. This usually comes as a shock to the student, as his tendency is often the reverse of the pillar he thought he was on.

In the light of what he has seen, the aspirant might then begin to perceive the parallels yet deeper within his own psyche, of active and passive attitudes and their response to himself, other people and situations. From these insights a picture of his own inner world should start to clarify as he detects the masculine and feminine aspects of each sefirah that composes his Yeziratic Tree. It is possible, for example, suddenly to realize that his emotional judgements tend to take the initiative, thereby making him jump to conclusions, or that his Nezah is passive, losing him the power to implement the ideas that are reverberating in an active Hod. With the aid of Tiferet and his maggid, he should be able to correct these imbalances and learn how to switch each sefirah into a male or female status. To do this takes time and requires much practice to be able to recognize, by an outer manifestation, what is going on deep in the psyche. This process is the conversion of the unconscious into the conscious, thereby gaining command, for the central column, over the mental mechanics which are worked by the automatic interaction of the male and female side pillars.

Above the orbit of personal consciousness lies the sphere of Self-consciousness centred in Tiferet. The circle enclosing the sefirot of Yesod, Hod, Nezah, Hesed, Gevurah and Daat includes the triad of the Soul, or Neshamah. With the detection of the male and female principle much insight can be gained into the nature of the Soul, if only by speculation through the literal approach. The Soul lies exactly between the upper and lower faces of the Yeziratic Tree, and as such is the mediator between the World of Beriatic Spirit and Asiyyatic Matter; as will be seen, it is in a neutral place between the masculine upper face and the feminine lower face, which is a vertical application of the active and passive roles. The attachment of the Soul Triad to the two outer pillars gives it the horizontal polarization, so that the Soul can participate as an activator below or a receptor above. In Kabbalistic Work it often performs both roles simultaneously, as the process of receiving and imparting flows down the Tree. This unique quality can be easily discerned by the simple logic of the Tree's design, which is another form of literal approach.

Taking the male and female principle up a stage higher, what has been discovered below in the physical world can be applied above and within a man to spiritual work. Bringing the Great Mother of Binah and the Great Father of Hokhmah into the consciousness of the aspirant is part of the task, for the closer Adam and Eve can be brought together, the greater the harmony within the Kabbalist. Tradition has it that the marriage between our primary parents is not always harmonious. Sometimes they are back to back and sometimes only one of them faces the other. One of the objectives of the Kabbalist is to bring the heavenly King and Queen face to face so that a conception may take place. On the level of the body this happens when male and female are mated under the right conditions, and the Will of God, descending the central column, passes through all the Worlds to bring about a fertilization in Asiyyah. A similar process occurs in Yezirah, with the fructification of a Soul from the potential seed of a Neshamah. It is called a rebirth by some traditions and is accomplished by the conversion and lifting of consciousness from the Second Garden to the Third Garden of the Extended Tree. Such a happening is the result of Work from below and Grace from above, with the male and female principles operating horizontally and vertically within an individual's psychological Tree. The next step is the conception of the Spirit, which manifests in the Daat of Yezirah, which is also the Yesod of Beriah. It is here, just between and below the Adam and Eve of the psyche, that the event occurs, as the inner male and female of a person meet in spiritual consummation.

For the aspirant who has been sent on this literal mission much new knowledge may be gained. By examining the factual and phenomenal world about him he should have learnt something about the noumenal realm that lies out of sight of the physical eye, thus following the Talmudic injunction on how to observe the invisible. In his subsequent work with the maggid the material is slowly transformed by the student from the physical to the psychological and then to the spiritual, so that he begins to experience what the male and female parts of himself are and how they function. He will then begin to perceive their operation within all Mankind and indeed throughout all the Worlds. In perhaps one such glimpse he will know who Adam and Eve are and what it really means, when the Bible says 'male and female created He them'. It is in such moments that the literal is transformed into the mystical, and the Bride of Malkhut receives the Bridegroom of Keter.

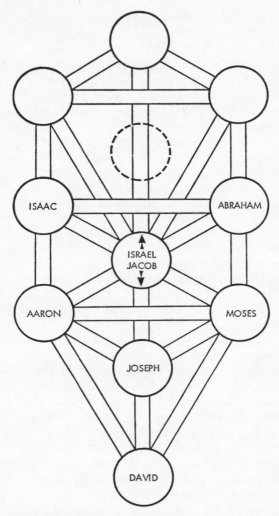

Figure 19. The Seven Shepherds. *The Patriarchs' lives and characters are seen by Kabbalists as allegories of the seven lower sefirot. With David as the worldly man at Malkhut and Joseph as the steward at Yesod, Jacob completes the central column as the person who transforms his being from the lower face into the upper as Israel. Aaron and Moses act as the priest and prophet, that is, the passive and active intermediaries, while Isaac and Abraham worship and act from Fear and Love of God.*

20
Allegorical

The second method by which an aspirant is trained is that of allegory. In the exercise that follows, the Biblical patriarchs are set out on the Tree. Known as the Seven Shepherds, their lives are said to express the various lower sefirot, and to the Kabbalist, their placing not only gives much insight into them, but a grand Biblical design on the stages of spiritual growth and the inner world of Yeziratic psychology.

Beginning with Malkhut the symbol of King David is used to exemplify the man who, despite his powerful animal nature, has a direct connection with the upper Worlds. His defeat of the giant Goliath is an allegory of his faith in God in dealing with the body and ego, although he did periodically succumb to his passions, as in his relationship with Uriah's wife Bathsheba. And yet out of this union came Solomon, which indicates the conversion of an apparent sin to a possibility of spiritual growth. Because he forgot himself and the Lord, David was not allowed to build the Temple, although his physical efforts gave his son the security and wealth to be able to accomplish the task. It is also interesting to note that David, whose name means 'the man after God's own heart', usurped the throne of the first king of Israel, Saul: yet another act of conversion from the purely animal state to that of one with some Foundation in the next World. According to tradition, out of the line of David the Messiah would be born. Seen Kabbalistically, this line is the central column stretching between Earth and Heaven. This pillar, named the One of Holiness, is the axis of ascending consciousness and of descending Will and Grace or Barakhah.

The next step up the Yeziratic Tree is Yesod, which is occupied by Joseph, the symbol of the ego. His name means 'He will add or increase'. As the son of Rachel he was especially favoured not only by Jacob, who presented him with a coat of many colours, but by nature, in his extraordinary good looks and gifts. This caused much trouble with his brothers, especially when Joseph saw in a dream how they would bow down to him. Because of this vanity, the ego Joseph, despite his special relationship to the Self his father, was sent down into Egypt to be sold as a slave in the lower face of Asiyyah. Here is a perfect allegorical description of the function and faults of Yesod: when ego claims primacy, it soon finds itself in trouble. In the case of Joseph this was a youthful misdemeanour of inexperience. In Egypt he was a good and loyal servant, for he rejected the advances of his master's wife, indicating a maturity and control of the sexual aspect of Yesod. This power is a considerable part of ego dynamic and image. In prison his skill in interpreting dreams gained him a favour and relative freedom when he explained the meaning of Pharaoh's dreams. Here the thin and good ears of corn, and the lean and fat kine, represented years of Mercy and then of Severity, or abundance and famine in the vegetable and animal levels of Asiyyah. After the interpretation, Joseph recommended that a man with discretion and wisdom should be set over Egypt, to store the surplus grain and cattle and so bring about a balance between the two outer pillars of the economic Tree of Egypt. Pharaoh thereupon appointed Joseph to the post, gave him his ring of authority and arrayed him in fine vestments, placing a gold chain about his neck. That is while he was still a servant, he was now the highest in the land, riding in the second state chariot after Pharaoh. Soon Joseph acquired an Egyptian wife (that is, adopted a persona), and through his influence brought his father and family down into Egypt where they could live a physical existence. This is precisely the situation and function of the ego as intermediary between the natural World of Asiyyah and the inner world of the Self. Provided that the ego acts as the devoted servant it may safely acquire and enjoy finery, status and education;

but its highly responsible position places it in the way of many temptations and habits that have to die out in the desert of Sinai that stretches
between Yesod and Tiferet.

In the Tree of the Seven Shepherds Moses and Aaron are placed at
Hod and Nezah. Here they are treated as two brothers or functional
complements, Aaron in the passive function of Hod and Moses in the
active role of Nezah. Aaron was noted for his eloquence, a talent of
Hod the sefirah of communication. He was also given the role of
priest; that is, he as the sefirah at the base of the column of Form represented the pillar of Tradition, as against Moses the prophet who acted
from the pillar of Revelation. These two side columns are the balance
to the Way that rises and descends the central pillar. In Kabbalah the
left pillar of Aaron is called Justice. It takes its quality from the passive
and rigorous sefirot of Binah, Gevurah and Hod. Without the complement of the active pillar the Tradition would be a hard set of rules
and severe disciplines. On the other hand, if the pillar of Revelation
were not contained by Tradition, the Work would become outlandish
and unacceptable at the Yesodic level of the Children of Israel, into
which Hod and Nezah flow. This is the functional relationship between
the two brothers, in their position between the Teaching above and
the Children of Israel below them in the Wilderness.

The central column of Holiness is the Way. Or at least it leads up
to the beginning of the Way at Tiferet. The task of Moses and Aaron
was to guide the Children of Israel to the Promised Land; but both
made vital mistakes; Aaron in agreeing to the Golden Calf and Moses
in an incident at Kadesh where he did not uphold the Lord's Holiness
to the Children of Israel. This cost them both their chance to enter the
Holy Land. Kabbalistically it reveals the level of Hod and Nezah
placed halfway between Yesod and Tiferet. They are confined to
operating in the transition zone of the threshold of ego-consciousness
and Self-consciousness that is stretched between them along the path
joining Hod and Nezah. In psychological terms this is when the
theoretical instruction coming from Aaron and the practice performed
by Moses starts to lift the aspirant Child of Israel up to the frontier
dividing the desert from the Promised Land. It is interesting to note
that the Israelites twice encamped at Kadesh, which means 'sacred'
and 'unusual', and twice were turned away from entering the Holy
Land even though they were on its very border. This describes the
moments of attainment and the flaws that make the aspirant turn back
into the desert again to continue his process of purification.

Moses and Aaron helped to bring the Children of Israel up out of. Egypt with the aid of the pillar of fire and cloud on the central column Their task is still to help all natural wayfarers and wanderers or Evrim, the Hebrew name for the Hebrews. From being nomads and slaves without a country, that is seekers without a place in the mundane world, the Israelites were led to their real home. This was the Land promised to Jacob and Isaac and Abraham, who form the Triad of the Soul.

Isaac and Abraham, like Moses and Aaron, complement each other, but at the emotional level of Gevurah and Hesed. Isaac worshipped God from fear and Abraham from love. Abraham was the friend of God and Isaac his dutiful follower. These aspects manifest in the test and act of devotion. Abraham's trial was to be required to sacrifice Isaac. Because of his love of God and Isaac's submission, both came through the ordeal into a special relationship to their Maker. So it is with the Triad of Charity composed of Gevurah, Hesed and Tiferet. These three sefirot are the elements of the Soul or Neshamah. Together they occupy the zone between the Nefresh of the natural man and the Ruah of the Spirit, whose habitat for incarnate man is the lower face of Beriah, the World of Creation. As the emotional balance between the tempering of discipline and the nurturing of devotion, Isaac and Abraham support Jacob, who stands at the Gate to the House of Israel. They may also be seen as the two angelic beings who guard and guide the Way into Upper Eden that was cut off from Adam and Eve when they descended into the natural world.

Isaac is that part of oneself that exercises Judgement and Abraham Mercy. Psychologically, this may be seen as the passive emotional complexes that retain and conserve, as against the active attitudes that open up and expand the emotional world. Anyone with a strong Isaac tends to be one of tight discipline, very rarely stepping out of what is the traditional line. The person with a powerful Abraham is more attractive, but he can sometimes be a little overbearing in his ebulliance. Balance is always necessary. It is interesting to observe that the Lightning Flash, as it proceeds down the Tree, comes upon Abraham first, giving him his revelations before it passes on to Isaac on the pillar of Form. The impulse then moves on to the third great patriarch, Jacob, at Tiferet.

The position of Jacob before he became Israel was that he possessed the birthright, but had yet to establish it in Tiferet. For seven years he worked in his uncle Laban's employ, not just for wages, but for the beautiful Rachel. To his surprise he was given Leah, her elder and less desirable sister: that is, he had to accept the disagreeable as well as the agreeable part of his training. However, because he loved Rachel so deeply, he was prepared to work another seven years and complete his covenant. In this way he also paid the debt incurred by having taken Esau's place as firstborn.

Jacob's journeymanship was not unprofitable from his point of view. While he had to contend with the domestic problems of his wives, that is, psychological crises of both an inner and outer nature, he did become wealthy with the Lord's aid, despite Laban's efforts to swindle him. (One must be as wise as a serpent as well as innocent as a dove, said one maggid.) His parting from his father-in-law began the initiation of his mastership, which was symbolized in his wrestling match with the angel.

On his return to Canaan, Jacob was faced with a meeting with his brother Esau. This was part of his test. He called on God to protect him and sent his family on ahead, leaving himself utterly alone. That night he wrestled with a man. The Bible gives no description beyond this, but it was obviously no ordinary mortal. They wrestled till day-break, until the man said 'Let me go', but Jacob replied, 'I will not let thee go, except thou bless me.' The man asked Jacob his name and said, 'Thy name shall be called no more Jacob, but Israel: for as a prince hast thou power with God and with men.' That is, Jacob had risen to make contact with the upper and have command over the lower parts of himself. Jacob then asked the man his name, but the Being would not give it to him. He had not risen to the Ultimate yet. However, the Being blessed him, that is the Barakhah of Grace flowed down from the Worlds above and transformed Jacob into Israel. One of the root meanings of Israel is 'He who has wrestled with God'.

The name and title of prince are not given lightly in the Bible. A person has to be what he is called. Israel, after the initiation was over, named the place Peniel, 'the Face of God', because he had met his Maker and still lived. This is the capacity of Tiferet. Moses could only see up the path from Nezah to Tiferet, a flank or hind part of God, as the Bible puts it. He was still despite his gift of prophecy a natural man confined, with Aaron his sefirotic counterpart, to the Sinai desert below. Even less could the unprepared Children of Israel confront the Divine from the level of Yesod. This is why they were instructed not to come up the mountain.

Jacob's conversion into Israel reveals three levels. The first is that Jacob the physical man, is the Keter of Asiyyah, the Crown of the body.

The second is that the conversion concerns the Tiferet of Yezirah, the Self of the psyche; and the third that this is the place of the Malkhut of Beriah the Kingdom of Heaven. The meaning is that in a fully developed Self there are three Worlds present. Here is the place where men, angels and God meet. The Being who wrestled with Jacob still awaits his match, for every aspirant will have his own Peniel where 'I' and 'Thou' meet face to face.

Here then, in personification and parable, is Mankind's situation, each Biblical personage and event rich in symbolism and information about the Worlds, sefirot, pillars, triads and paths: thus for the Kabbalist the Bible is an allegory of Existence and Mankind's Divine and Cosmic purpose.

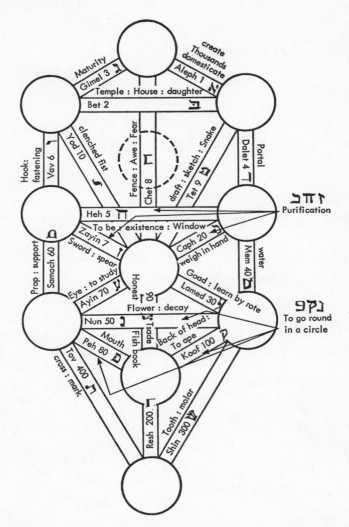

Figure 20. Hebrew Letters and Paths. *In metaphysical studies Kabbalah uses the Hebrew alphabet in a number of ways. In the illustrated scheme each path is given a letter, the combinations of adjacent paths and triads making up words that give clues or confirmations to ideas. Such complex methods require not only much background information but an impeccable intellectual integrity.*

21
Metaphysical

According to the *Oxford Dictionary* metaphysics is the theoretical philosophy of being and knowing. In Kabbalah this covers a vast field of studies ranging from cosmogony, or the origin of the Universe, through the dynamics of the Tree, the patterns of numbers, symbols of letters, angelology and the study of the working of Providence and Fate, to the nature of God's Attributes. At this instructional stage it is obvious that the maggid would not give the aspirant any task too far beyond his capability. His object is to train the aspirant how to learn. This skill is the key to all the theories and practices he will have to master; therefore the chief purpose of the metaphysical method at this point is to learn how to think.

The Universe is based on order; its basic pattern is summed up in the Laws embodied in the Sefirotic Tree. The Tree at first sight is a rigid structure, but as study and experience increase, the rigidity of the diagram begins to dissolve as the subtleties of its dynamics start to emerge. Gradually, as the aspirant comes to appreciate the interaction of Laws, the flows, circulations, interchanges, transformations and levels, the Tree becomes less and less like an external abstraction and more like a living organism. When it has begun to be part of the aspirant's own being, he can say that he knows something of Kabbalah. Until then he must work continuously with the theory and practice of metaphysics.

The Sefirotic Tree of Life is the key to Kabbalah. Therefore the first thing the aspirant has to do is acquaint himself with its principles, as has been done at the beginning of this and other books. However it must be more than just a set of notes on the Tree and its dynamics. The scheme must be built up of realities, so that it has a personal significance. This is done by the maggid taking the aspirant, or indeed the whole group, slowly up the Tree, step by step. Here is one method. Beginning with Malkhut, the maggid explains that this is the elemental level of the Tree. It is the place into which all the paths flow and resolve, so that Malkhut, the Kingdom, contains all the Force, Form and Consciousness inherent in the sefirot, pillars, triads and paths. Such a concentration makes Malkhut the passive pole to the positive source of Keter the Crown. In terms of Asiyyah, where most people exist and have their consciousness, this concentration is manifest in the Elements of four states of Matter. Contained in Earth, Water, Air and Fire are the four material expressions of the Four Worlds, the active and passive pillars and all the other laws. At this point the maggid sends the group out to observe and collect all they can about the nature of Malkhut.

The following week they return and present their findings. One person brings a diagram of the human body and its constituents, showing the various solids, liquids and gases needed to keep it alive. Fire could be taken as heat or the electrical activity in the body. Another person lights a candle and points to the solid wax, the melted liquid being burnt and the gas, heat and light coming off the flame. The candle, one of the most commonly used implements of religion, contains the essence of the Manifest Universe, utilizing all four states of Matter. It is the perfect Malkhutian symbol. A third person produces a flower. Here a life principle has transformed earth and water into cell tissue with the aid of air and light. Remove any one of these elements and the flower will die before its allotted span. Moreover, it is observed, the plant contains the world of Yezirah, in that it is slowly changing form, through bud and bloom, to be overblown and finally withered by death. And further, it has within this cycle the idea of the perfect flower, the concept being within Beriah where the original flower of all that species was created. The whole operation, the student concludes, is an expression of Azilut, so that it is indeed possible to see the nature of Manifest Existence in the Malkhut of a common plant.

The following week Yesod is studied, each member of the group bringing in an object, perhaps a poem, or an idea that illuminates the sefirah. One man shows a picture of himself in his favourite outfit. This is his yesodic image of himself. Another brings a print-out sheet from a computer, explaining that one of Yesod's functions is to act as a screen upon which the upper sefirot project their influx. Someone else mimes the gestures of anger and pleasure to illustrate how Yesod reflects the inner state, and another holds the group spellbound as he tells a fable rich in imagery. This power, he concludes, can be a strength or a weakness in Yesod.

At the next meeting the group studies the paired sefirot of Hod and Nezah. This task is not quite so easy, as they begin to move out of ordinary experience. Hod and Nezah are halfway between Asiyyah and Yezirah. They serve as the active and passive initiators and receptors for the body and the lower psyche. Hod, for example, is the principle that governs all communications within the body. These are the impulses within the nervous system and the chemical messengers of metabolism as well as the power of speech and the ability to see, hear, smell and touch. Nezah in the body acts as the driving force within the organs. It makes the heart pump and the lungs expand and contract. Without Nezah there would be no energy in the body, nor would there be the regular rhythms vital to its maintenance, for Nezah means Eternity, that is ever repeating. Together they make a check and balance between energy and matter, the left side holding the limits while the right deals with the input and output. Should one sefirah be defective, the body will either slow down or go too fast. In a chronic state this can develop into atrophy on the Form side or cancer, or uncontrolled Force or growth, on the other.

All these exercises indicate, point and illustrate some sense of what the sefirot are about. One can never actually pinpoint any one of them; if one does then it is not true. The nature of the sefirot is that they are principles, and the only way the aspirant can approach them is through their manifestation in the lower Worlds. As yet, at this level, the study has to be confined to Asiyyah and the frontier of Yezirah, the psychological world. However, as one works up the Tree, a dim picture of the nature of and difference between the sefirot begins to emerge.

The first part of the metaphysical exercise has been working from the visible towards the invisible; but there is also the reverse method. In Kabbalah there are many abstract formulae that have no meaning unless one knows something already. The Sefer Yezirah or the Book of Formations is a prime example. This book, probably written in the early years of the Common Era, is a textbook on Kabbalistic theory, a metaphysical primer. For example, in one passage it speaks of the three primordial mothers of Water, Air and Fire. These are given the three Hebrew letters of Mem, Aleph and Shin. They are then placed in six combinations, or 'sealed in six wings', as the writer puts it. These letter combinations describe the interactions of active Shin or Fire, passive Mem or Water and neutral Aleph or Air principles at work. While no doubt impressive to those who love to accumulate useless information, they are a meaningless set of equations unless one is familiar with the Sefirotic Tree.

According to one tradition, Fire is the symbol of the right pillar and Water of the left, with Air being the element of the central column. Earth is seen as Malkhut below, and the fifth element Ether above at Keter. The interaction of the three primordial letters also describes the tripartite roles of each sefirah, so that, say, Gevurah can within its own field be not only passive but active and even neutral. Thus, while Judgement is basically a passive or Mem-Water function in response to what is presented to it, it can act and mete out severity, which it does if a law is continually broken. The Talmud says that if a man commits an evil act then yet more occasion for evil arises, until he is so evil that the Universe turns on him with the severity of natural justice in order to push him back into equilibrium. Here is the sefirah of Gevurah in an active or Shin-Fire role. In a neutral or Aleph-Air state Gevurah might take up quite a different role in at least three triads; the top one with Binah and Tiferet, the middle with Hesed and Tiferet and the lowest with Tiferet and Hod. Here it may be no more than the just mediator in matters of understanding (Binah) of truth (Tiferet) and of communication (Hod). As will be noted, all the triads in the Tree are connected to the central column. This means there is not only a direct affiliation with the predominantly Air of neutral pillar, but the presence of Consciousness and Will. In this way metaphysics can never be removed from experience.

Returning to the letters, there are in Kabbalah several systems besides that of the Sefer Yezirah which use the Hebrew alphabet to explain theories or be put into practice. These may include the use of numbers, because the Aleph-Bet is also a numerical system as well as being the name root of each letter from which many words spring. Perhaps the most familiar fact is that there are twenty-two letters in the Hebrew alphabet, one for each of the twenty-two channels or paths joining the sefirot on the Tree. On the studies of numbers and roots there are vast tracts written over the centuries, and even today some Kabbalists still probe into the number and meaning of letters and words in the Bible, seeking clues and keys in mathematical connections and parallels. An example of Gematria, or the number-word connection, is the numerical value of the name of the archangel Metatron and the Divine Name S H A D D A I, both of which add up to the same total of 314. This is seen by some Kabbalists as highly significant, as are many other numerical connections throughout the Bible. As said, there are many ways of working in Kabbalah, as long as the intent is directed to God; otherwise it is no more than a Hodian exercise.

The example system of letter metaphysics to be discussed here is based on the progression of the Lightning Flash completing the triads as it descends the paths connecting the emerging sefirot and allowing the Worlds to unfold from Azilut to Asiyyah in an orderly sequence. It is said in the Tradition that there are thirty-two paths, that is ten sefirot and twenty-two letters. Between them they bring the Universe into Manifest Existence. The ten sefirot are objective, while the paths which correspond to the twenty-two letters are subjective; the former are basically unchanging, the latter are variables. In this manner there is a subtle and complex interplay within the Tree. For example, a positive impulse from Nezah can travel up any one of five different paths. Let us suppose it goes down the one to Yesod. Here it starts a quite different circulation pattern from one going down the path to Malkhut. In the Nezah-Yesod impulse the flow goes on down to Malkhut and then up to return to Nezah, while all the adjacent triads follow the path flows initiated by the original impulse of Nezah to Yesod. This affects the whole Tree, clearly demonstrating that nothing occurs in the Universe without the total being affected (see Fig. 21). Here is the basis of the argument for and against man's good and evil intent and actions. It also demonstrates the theoretical and metaphysical premise of advanced Kabbalistic Work in influencing the Worlds above and below.

The letters on the paths and their root meanings help to define the characteristics of each path. Thus the path between Hod and Nezah, given the letter Nun, means to 'flower and decay'. This describes graphically the quality of the impulse coming from either sefirah. For instance, any sense data like that of sight or hearing is passed from Hod to Nezah. The sound enters Hod through Malkhut, the body, and is responded to by Nezah, the impulse of which will turn the head round.

The sound then fades until the next waves. If this phenomenon of flowering and decay did not occur, our eyes would see the same fixed image of the scene we saw at birth. As it happens, the process of flowering and decaying, or in this case of manifestation, the flow of electronic impulses down the optic nerve, is continuous so that we get a moving picture, each frame a fraction of a second long. As part of the universal scheme the principle designated by the letter Nun is vital. Without it nothing could be received or imparted on the frontier between Asiyyah and Yezirah. In the body it is the crucial function that divides the membrane levels between organs and tissue, and in the psyche the liminal threshold where the 'flowering and decaying' is seen as the rising and sinking of thoughts and feelings across the line between consciousness and the unconscious.

Another way in which the letters are used in relation to the Tree is to read them as triads. Here they form three-letter root words. An example of this is produced by the triad Hod-Nezah-Yesod whose adjoining paths and their letters make the Hebrew root word 'nakoof' which means 'to go round in a circle'. This is a very precise description of this triad, as the observation of daydreams or worries, with their lack of connection with the reality of Tiferet within and the reality of Malkhut below, indicates. Another triad, that of Gevurah-Tiferet-Hesed, forms the root word for 'purification and cleansing'. This gives much insight into the nature and work of the Charity triad of the Soul.

The study of the letters and the paths is a complex metaphysical exercise in itself. It contains layer upon layer of depth within the context of the total Tree. Kept at a purely academic level it is, and has often proved, a blind alley. For the Kabbalist it must be put to practical use. It must be made to help Heaven reach Earth and Earth to reach Heaven. Without this aim all the Work is pointless. Therefore let us begin to convert metaphysics into experience.

The path between Malkhut and Yesod is lettered Resh, that is, the head or beginning. The path between Yesod and Tiferet is called 'honesty' or the 'just man', the Zadek, after the letter Tsade placed there. The middle path stretching beyond Tiferet passes through the Triad of Purification and crosses the Gevurah-Hesed path of Heh which means 'to be' and 'window'. This vertical path, the longest on the Tree, is given the letter Chet, which is the root of the words 'fence' and 'awe'. It moves into and out of Daat the non-sefirah of Knowledge and the Holy Spirit, and passes on to Keter the Crown, Source of All Existence.

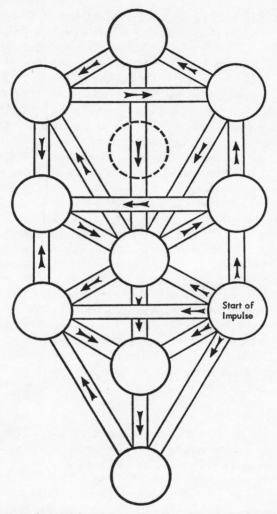

Figure 21. Circulation Flow. *Here the effect of an impulse from Nezah is seen in the resultant flows about the Tree. Nor is this pattern the only one possible from the same input. Thus with many configurations of flow from each sefirah being possible, a vast range of subtleties can be generated. The complexity of a single situation in ordinary life demonstrates this well.*

To begin to comprehend what all this means one must have covered a considerable amount of ground. Kabbalah is not a quick process of enlightenment. It involves patient and thorough preparation even before the Work proper can begin. So far it has been principally a matter of getting the sefirot of Malkhut, Yesed, Hod and Nezah into balance. Now comes the task of completing the lower face by opening up the path of the Zadek between Yesod and Tiferet. This requires the development of will.

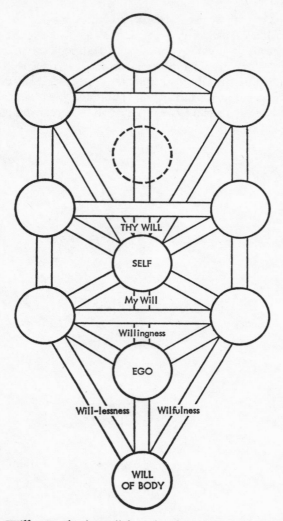

THY WILL

SELF

My Will

Willingness

EGO

Will-lessness   Wilfulness

WILL
OF BODY

Figure 22. Will. *Besides the Will descending from above there are various wills operating from below. In this Tree the types of will an evolving person has to contend with are set out. To recognize these different wills is vital for the Kabbalist because they can assert pressure on a man without his knowledge. This can thwart spiritual growth.*

22
Will

While one may possess much theory and have done much practice it is useless unless it is realized upon the middle column of consciousness. This requires will. As there are several levels of consciousness so there are several levels of will and these must be recognized before any knowledge of Kabbalah becomes real.

Most natural men possess no will. That is, they possess no will of their own, but are governed by wills arising out of the Asiyyatic Tree. The most powerful of these influences is the will of the body. As a vegetable organism it must absorb and excrete, for example, and if it is not allowed to do so it exerts all its will with considerable persuasive power. In most people's lives the body plays a dominant part not only in the basic demands of food or rest, but in the need to fulfil the animal desires such as being attractive and sociable. Although these preoccupations make a man or woman personable, they have little to do with individual will. They are the workings of Nature's will to bring the sexes together.

On the Yeziratic Tree, the will of the body rises up the three paths radiating from Malkhut to influence the lower face of the psyche. On the right it stimulates, on the left it constrains, while in the middle it balances as a general sense of physical well-being. If there is a malfunction on either side, the middle column connecting the central nervous system of Malkhut to the Yesod of the psyche is informed of it by the Daat of the body. With the influx of pain or discomfort the person sets about finding a remedy: for example he drinks a soothing alkaline mixture to balance an over-active acid in the stomach. Here is the Tree of Asiyyah exerting its will on Yezirah.

At the Yeziratic Yesod is ego. This is the Foundation of the psyche. As the simultaneous Daat of Asiyyah it provides an image of the body. In most people this physical picture is far more clear and organized than the one they have of their psyche, because in the natural state their Yesod is composed of a hotch-potch of disconnected fragments based on education, environment and social custom. Few people really know themselves, although they have a vague image of what they may be like. This is often only a mirage generated by what they want to be, how others see them, and the masks that society makes them put on in order to be accepted. Under these conditions there is no real will in the ego because it is too subject to other influences, such as the body and pressures coming from the community. However it does exhibit what appears to be manifestations of will. These on examination divide into three aspects, each associated with the three pillars.

The first is the phenomenon of will-lessness. Here the passive side of the ego simply responds to those elements in its Foundation that are on the side of Form. One man, for example, will not openly go against his colleagues over an issue like a strike, which would place him outside the majority. He conforms because he identifies the image of himself with that of the others in his union. This identity, as a doctor or a miner, may be all that a man has to cling to if he has no real individuality.

The second aspect is wilfulness. This is generated by the active side of Yesod. Here different parts of the ego assert themselves, often against each other's interest, because in most people the ego is not a uniform entity but an unconnected kaleidoscope of attitudes, postures and ideas which ego-consciousness invests with life when the attention is directed on and into them. An instance of this is the person who demands social justice and yet is a tyrant in his own home. Wilfulness can also be the exhibitionist, rebel complement or opponent to the passive will-lessness side. It depends on which side of the Tree is the strongest at any given moment.

Another reason for the lack of real will in the ego is illusion. Yesod is called the non-luminous mirror because it merely reflects. However, what is seen in the mirror can be, and usually is, believed to be the real thing. This is made more complex because the mirror of the ego is coloured and sometimes distorted by the type of experience we have encountered during our formative years. Thus, rich and poor individuals may have totally differing outlooks on the world and on themselves even though they may have been brought up in the same small village. An example of no real will is that a person may simply imagine who he is, and live out his life according to what he and others expect of him. Such an illusion can prevent him from ever becoming a real person. Indeed it is sometimes a strange quirk in history that an employer has in his employ a man who is his spiritual superior. Many kings frozen in their public image were dependent upon their sages.

The proper state of the ego is willingness; its function is to serve the Self at Tiferet. In natural man this does not happen, so that he possesses no coordinated or individual will despite the belief that he is the master of his own life. In Kabbalah the aspirant, acknowledging his lack of Self-will, initially relies on the maggid to perform as his Tiferet, in order to teach Yesod how to hear instruction from within and above. This means he has to consent to be willing, and so prepare to obey. However, it is not an easy task, because the Zadek path between Yesod and Tiferet is the place where one's personal devil 'lies in wait', the other name for this path. In Kabbalah this devil is called the Adversary, and it is what might be called at this stage the 'dark side' of the ego. One's personal devil is made up of those disparate parts which form a negative ego. Such a disjointed entity can assume rulership of Yesod by ego-worship. Often this entity is the king of the situation because it thrives in the egocentric world that created it. However, when the direct will of Tiferet or, worse, the outside will of the maggid intrudes to remodel, control and direct the Yesodic Foundation, the dark side of the ego starts to fight a battle to preserve its sovereignty. Now, the symbol for the devil is a creature made up of all sorts of different parts. It is usually depicted as ugly. This, however, is very misleading because in the psychological World of Yezirah it can take on many forms, especially when it is fighting for identity-survival. Sometimes, for example, the dark side of the ego will use the very terms the aspirant is learning to continually turn the clock back. It will project the pleasant illusion of remarkable progress, which is not at all difficult in the period of transition between the dissolution of the old Yesodic image of the world and the new Foundation. The work of the

Adversary is an ever-present threat to the Work of Kabbalah, and both the aspirant and the maggid must always be watchful.

Out of willingness comes the acceptance of discipline. Discipline means 'to follow', and in Kabbalah it is not the maggid who is followed but the laws of the Tree and their application within the Tradition. One law we have already noted is the relationship between the Yesod of the aspirant and the acting role of the Tiferet of the maggid. This enables the aspirant to learn how to obey, or to be more precise, teaches his Yesod to take up its correct role as servant to Tiferet. When the time comes, the maggid ceases to be the aspirant's Seat of Solomon and the man takes on the full responsibility for himself. Meanwhile he has to abide by the rules of the group, which aids his Tiferet and exposes the ego's dark side when it does not wish to comply with the group's requirements, or the man's ultimate good. An example of the application of a law at several levels is the rule of reliability.

Reliability in Kabbalah indicates a true stability in a person between the right and left pillars. Any tendency to over-enforce rules, or obey them slavishly, reveals an imbalance. The Way of Kabbalah is Knowledge. That is, to know what one is doing and why. Therefore at first the reason for a rule is explained by the maggid, although sometimes it is not understood until months, and sometimes years later. The rule is then implemented as a general principle that can be applied in many ways. These may include carrying out certain duties for the group, such as buying the bread and wine, taking notes or washing dishes. In ordinary social or family matters the ego might protest or quietly side-step the task, but in the group the rule not only fulfils a practical function but serves as an exercise in dealing with will-lessness and wilfulness. The voluntary submission of the ego is a vital training: one has to know how to serve before one can command.

Another application of the rule of reliability is the test of going where one is told. In this a person may be instructed to be at a certain place at a very inconvenient time. If he really values Kabbalah, he will soon vanquish the objections of the ego's dark side and go, no matter what the time or the distance involved. This not only helps to develop the will connection with Tiferet but separates out those who have no real, serious commitment to the Work. This is very necessary because a person who backs away here is wasting his and the maggid's time.

The development of the will of Tiferet is a key skill in Kabbalah. Therefore the training begins early. One of the first practices, after the initial theory stage has been fed into Yesod, is to remember and centre in the Self of Tiferet as often as possible. It is not an easy exercise, because normally it occurs spontaneously, perhaps a hundred times in a lifetime, so distracting is the hurly burly of the Asiyyatic world and the preoccupation of the ego with itself. Because the natural state cannot be satisfactorily relied on to produce the right conditions, special situations have to be devised. On the orthodox side of a Tradition the ritual of the religious service raises the Yesodic level of consciousness by creating a conducive atmosphere for Tiferet to be contacted. These conditions, however, are not maintained day in and day out, except in a religious community such as a monastery or Hasidic society, which runs a continuous cycle of prayer. Therefore for the Kabbalist, who has to work in the world, a special set of reminders has to be provided until he reaches the point where, as one maggid said, 'Kabbalah is whatever I am doing at the time.'

One of the techniques used to remind the aspirant of his will, is the method of remembering the other members of his group at, say, ten in the morning, at noon and at three in the afternoon. At these times, no matter what he is doing, he must recall the faces and names of all present at the last meeting. The effect is to shift him out of ego consciousness, up the Zadek path and into Tiferet. This act of will cannot but make him realize who he is, where he is and why he is doing it. Such a moment of coming upon oneself is sometimes quite startling, because it reveals the twilight world of Yesod where we spend most of our time neither in Heaven nor on Earth. Indeed, the number of times he remembers to perform the task is a good indication of the state of his progress, and this he has to report honestly, as do the others, to the meeting. To lie about the omissions, moreover, is to break contact with himself rather than with the group or maggid, because the Zadek path cannot be trodden by the dishonest. Another direct benefit of this particular exercise is that, at the moment of remembering, the aspirant draws on the Charity Triad of the group. In the emotional connection of the mutual consciousness, he links with the Selves of all the other members, and so they aid each other, despite the distance between them. This strange experience of perceiving other people's presence is often the first glimpse the aspirant has of the power of will in the Yeziratic world.

It is important here to remember that the development of Self-will is not confined to esoteric disciplines. It is possible for a natural man to attain a Tiferet connection. Such men are natural individuals: that is, they have worked on their animal capability and devoted its passion sufficiently to reach the Keter of the Asiyyatic body, that is, the Self of Yezirah. Self-made men, as the name implies, may be found in the arts, sciences and industry. They occur in all the professions of war and peace, and indeed anywhere a natural individual can exert himself. The quality of such people is often larger than life, which is what they are, when compared to the scope of vegetable men; their hallmark is fate, because in relations to the mass their lives have a distinctive pattern which creates opportunities that most people miss through fear of change or through preoccupation with dreams. This is why, sometimes, the greatest villains can transform into saints. They have the will-power to do so.

For the aspirant the acquisition of individuality means the full responsibility for himself. When the maggid sees he has reached this point, he may send him away from the group. Certainly, from then on the maggid withdraws the rule of obeying his instructions. Indeed he might even provoke a situation where the aspirant has to take a stand in order to dissolve the link of obedience between them. More often than not, the aspirant is given the task of instructing those who have come after him, so that he pays his debt to the maggid by forging the next link in the chain of evolving generations.

From an allegorical point of view the aspirant is in the position of Jacob on leaving the household of Laban after he had completed the first part of his training. No longer a journeyman, the aspirant is his own master and can do as he pleases with his life, because he can now say 'This is my will'. The significance of such an event is often marked by an outward initiation which may take the form of a ceremony in which a declaration and a blessing are imparted and received. The ritual itself is based on the interplay of the two pillars, with the maggid at Tiferet bestowing the Barakhah flowing down from the upper Worlds to the disciple below. The act of acceptance raises the aspirant into direct connection with the House of Israel, so that he may draw on the left pillar of Tradition and upon the right pillar of Revelation.

Having received Kabbalah, he begins the inward initiation. The man is now in the situation of Jacob at Peniel. No longer reliant on the maggid, he is utterly alone – or is he? For out of the No-Thingness at the centre of the initiation emerges 'the likeness of a man'. There in the depths of his being, the Self struggles with the SELF, until in the darkness of Daat, between the Tiferet and Keter of Yezirah, the man meets the Divine face to face. This silent, still and unseen communion brings the Knower and the Known into a realization that converts the Tiferet of Yezirah into the coexistent Malkhut of Beriah. Jacob is transformed into Israel; from this moment of Knowledge in Daat, the Kabbalist begins to build a Foundation in the World of Creation. He has entered the Kingdom of Heaven, the first state of the seven levels of Teshuvah or Redemption in the World, of the Spirit where it is no longer my will, but Thy Will be done.

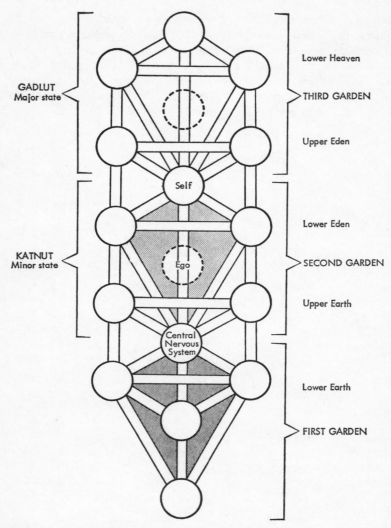

Figure 23. Gadlut and Katnut. *The major and minor states of consciousness occur throughout the Extended Tree, although they are initially perceived in moments of lucid awakening, as against ordinary consciousness. The Gadlut or major condition is essential to any Kabbalistic Work, because without direct contact with the self the upper Worlds remain remote.*

23
Minor and Major States

Although a person may have become a Kabbalist, he is by no means a fully developed man. Indeed his position is, in the words of one Kabbalist, 'a man reborn, not of the flesh [the lower face] but of the spirit [the upper face of the Yeziratic Tree]'. This places him in the situation of a babe in the Yesod of the Beriatic World where he has begun to form a Foundation. However this does not mean he has no obligations. As a person who has his own will, he has command over the lower Worlds within his being. He can control his animal and vegetable aspects, or at least not be dominated by them, so that they are rendered passive in relation to the psyche. Moreover, he can rule his Yesodic ego, and rise at will up the Zadek path to be in Tiferet. This achievement makes him responsible for himself and all his actions as regards other men and God. He can no longer declare ignorance of the Law. He knows, and knows that he knows. There is no excuse for misconduct, though of course to err is human.

Error occurs from forgetting, either intentionally or unintentionally. This comes about through wilfulness or will-lessness, and indicates a drop in the level of consciousness to the path between the ego and the body. An example of this in very ordinary circumstances is seen in a man who is trying to give up smoking. The body desires a cigarette, but it is opposed by the original promise made in Tiferet. The ego, placed between the Self and the body, can either implement the order of the upper will or ignore it and rationalize the will of the body into a semi-dream condition where the person suddenly finds himself with a cigarette in his mouth. The upper will may again remind him of his promise, but now the ego switches from will-lessness into wilfulness and still continues to let the body smoke.

This situation parallels the continuous struggle in spiritual development between the body, the ego and the Self, except that here the problem is not to deny something but to affirm it. The word 're-member' means precisely what it says: to re-member, to reconnect. The Kabbalist wants to recall himself, be in continuous contact with Tiferet of the Self so that he may participate in the three Worlds that meet there. To be only in the ego means to be immersed in Asiyyah, the state of Esau, who perceived only what he desired and had no thought of consequences. This state, alas, is the one in which most of us live; and even the new Kabbalist spends much of his time there, because even he has not totally mastered the worldly situation. It takes many years to enter fully the Promised Land. The inbred habits of slavery do not die off quickly.

In Kabbalah there is a recognition of two states of consciousness. The first is called Katnut, the minor condition, and the second Gadlut, the major condition. Katnut occurs when a man is in ego, that is, confined to the lower face of the Yeziratic Tree, and Gadlut is when he is in Tiferet, and has access to the upper face of Yezirah, which is also the lower face of Beriah. In terms of the Five Gardens or faces of the Extended Tree, Katnut is the condition of the Second and First Gardens from the bottom, that is the Lower and Upper Earths, the latter of which is also Lower Eden. The state of Gadlut applies to the Third Garden of Upper Eden, which corresponds simultaneously to the lower face of Heaven. Here we glimpse the potential of the two conditions.

The persistence of Katnut is considered unfortunate but inevitable, because Kabbalists realize that even evolving people cannot always maintain the condition of being in Tiferet. The Katnut state is generated by the demands of the outer world and its attractions and the pulls of the inner world with its vegetable and animal levels which continually assault a man, trying to remember himself, with their requirements. Therefore Kabbalists do not condemn a man for forgetting who he is, where he is and why he is there, but set it as a constant aim to be in the

Present as often as possible. This objective is always focused on the meeting in Tiferet between 'I' and 'Thou'. When a man is in Tiferet he will be conscious of God. Indeed, this exercise is embodied in the great prayer of the Shema which is recited at least three times a day. As noted, it begins *'Hear, O Israel'*: that is listen, awaken, pay attention, come into Tiferet. *'The Lord is our God'*: that is that SELF is the Self in all men's Selves. *'The Lord is One'*: that is there is in this state no separation, because in Tiferet is the essence of All, and All is One. The prayer goes on to instruct the person praying to commit himself with all his heart, soul and might to love God, so that no part of him, even as a natural man, is excluded from this commitment. This is emphasized by the injunction to hold these words in the heart (Tiferet) and to teach them diligently 'to thy children' which means not only one's natural offspring but to those lesser or lower parts of oneself such as the ego and the animal and vegetable souls. The prayer continues: 'And [thou] shalt talk of them [the opening words, *The Lord is our God. The Lord is One*] when thou sittest in thy house, and when thou walkest by the way, and when thou liest down and when thou risest up.' These lines may be seen both as a literal reminder to be in Tiferet always, even while about one's Asiyyatic business, or Kabbalistically, when one realizes that the House being spoken of is Israel and the Way the central column of Holiness, with the hint on Katnut and Gadlut expressed in the lines 'when thou liest down and when thou risest up'. After describing various aids and signs of reminder to be bound upon the heart and head, the prayer concludes that 'thou shalt write them [the words *The Lord is our God. The Lord is One*] upon the doorposts of thy house and upon thy gates'. This again points out the exit and entry place of Tiferet between upper and lower faces of the outer and inner Worlds. There are many such prayers which have more than their literal level, and which may be used in a devotional or a contemplative way. They are, in effect, a method of attaining access to Self-consciousness – the Gadlut condition.

A man may be in the Gadlut state for a fraction of a second. This is the moment of great lucidity that everyone experiences at some time in their lives. It may be for example in time of war, when a man suddenly sees that the difference between the quick and the dead is a matter of existing in different Worlds. It can come at the height of sexual passion, when two individuals dissolve not only into each other but altogether into a realization that there is no separation of anything from anything. Gadlut can occur when walking down a busy city

F

street, so that it is transformed into a timeless moment when the person perceives all the various journeys everyone in sight is making from the cradle to the grave. He may see in that instant why they are all there, on that day, in that street – for a reason far beyond their present knowledge. Such glimpses into Gadlut are a gift of Heaven. These acts of Grace descend often at a crucial time in a person's life, down from the upper part of his Tree to illuminate some question, point out a direction or confirm a conclusion by which he is puzzled. Often their significance is not fully recognized, and they remain merely remarkable experiences to be trotted out as unusual or odd, or even as moments of insanity. The uninjured man who walked away from an air crash in which everybody else was killed may not recognize the message that he has a job to do before he dies, whereas another man, who perhaps missed that same flight because of an unforeseen delay, might perceive he had been protected by Providence for a definite reason. It depends whether one is in Gadlut or Katnut.

In Kabbalah the objective is to be in Gadlut as often as possible, because when in touch with the Self, many possibilities are opened. From the sefirah of the Self radiate eight paths. Moreover these paths carry influxes from three different Worlds. The lower set, for example, are made up of the three uppermost paths of Asiyyah. All the eight operate from the Tiferet of Yezirah, while into the Beriatic aspect of the Self flows the influx of the three lowest paths of Creation. When such a combination focuses on this place where my will and Thy Will meet, miracles become feasible. A miracle is defined as an occasion when the laws of an upper World manifest in a lower one. This, however, is only possible if there is an intermediary vehicle to transform the influx from above to below. That is what Practical Kabbalah is about.

In the Katnut or the minor state, it is not possible for the upper Worlds to have any direct influence, except by an act of Grace. This gift, however, is only to help people to help themselves. Much can be done, for example, by a maggid to aid an aspirant, but the real work must be put in by the person himself, if he wishes to rise out of his old slave-minded condition. Should he insist on staying in the Sinai desert, nothing can be done for him until Providence provides a shock to move him on. For the aspirant who holds back, the Katnut state is neither Heaven nor Earth; if he cannot go back to Egypt, he must make great efforts to rise and obtain Gadlut, because to know as much as he does, without doing anything with it, can create a very special kind of Sinai desert hell. This sharp and barren state is the spur that

Providence uses. It may take the form of a disastrous relationship, where one's integrity is tested, or a period in which there appears to be no meaning or direction in anything with which one becomes involved. An act of Grace is not always one of Mercy; it sometimes comes from the pillar of Severity.

To be in Gadlut, the major state where three Worlds meet, is to reach the first state of Devekut. Devekut is the Kabbalistic name for Communion, that is direct affiliation with the Creator. This status is apparent from the position of the Self as the Beriatic Malkhut on the extended Tree, where the Kabbalist begins to form a permanent connection with the World of Creation.

It is a not uncommon experience, according to those who have had it, to sense, perceive or even directly to know that one is in the Presence of the Creator. It is expressed in Kabbalah in various ways from the already mentioned term 'Thou' to the 'Holy One, blessed be He'. Sometimes it is described by one of the several names for Tiferet – Adornment, which means a Presence of Infinite Beauty. Beauty, in fact, is merely the outer garment, the decoration of the Reality. No mortal man may see directly the Face of the Creator and continue to live, so he is granted to perceive a 'Likeness' of the perfect but unseen Presence that exists within the Manifest Universe. It is said that the Shekhinah, the Hebrew name for this Presence or the 'Dwelling', was in the burning bush that Moses saw, and that it hovered over the Tabernacle in Sinai and in the Holy of Holies in the Temple. It is also said that the Shekhinah accompanies Israel in its exile. All these allegorical situations point to the quality of the middle pillar of Holiness that stretches from the Crown of Crowns down through all the Worlds to the lowest Malkhut of Jacob's pillow of stone at the bottom of the Ladder. However, while the Shekhinah is present up through all the central sefirot of Asiyyah, it appears in the consciousness of a man only when he is in the Self, in the state of Gadlut and forms a direct link with the Holy Spirit. This is why it is said that the Shekhinah rests upon those who, however placed, are in continual rememberance of God. It is here, in the Devekut of the Self, that the Vilon or Veil is raised to reveal the Seat of Faith and the first of the seven Palaces of the Throne of Heaven.

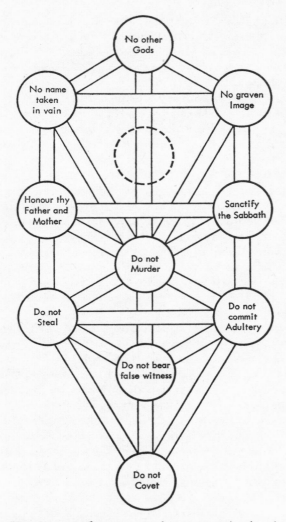

Figure 24. Ten Commandments. *As the Universe is based on the ten Attributes or utterances of God, so each Commandment is rooted in a sefirah. The Supernal triad of Keter-Hokhmah-Binah clearly demonstrates the instructions concerning Divinity, while the seven lower sefirot of Construction relate directly to Man.*

24
Neshamah: Soul

While a man may gain a glimpse of the Heavenly Palaces of Beriah from the Tiferet of Yezirah, he may not fully enter them until he has well and truly begun to purify the Yeziratic body of his psyche. This takes place in the Triad of the Soul.

So far we have studied the Asiyyatic Tree, which embodies the cellular vehicle and its vegetable and animal intelligence, and the mental mechanics of the natural man. We have also seen the arising out of Asiyyah of man seeking to evolve beyond the purely earthbound state. This has taken us into Yezirah, the World of the psyche. The psyche, as briefly described in Chapter 6, follows the pattern of the Sefirotic Tree, because all complete organisms at every level in Manifest Existence are based on its laws and design.

On the whole natural man experiences only the lower face of Yezirah. However he does, at least once in his life, get a glimpse of the upper face in a gift of Grace. To enter the upper face at will and view it for more than a flash requires as we have seen, much preparation and work. The establishment of a gate into the Third Garden of Jacob's Ladder is followed by a period of refinement which is necessary before a man can enter it properly, and explains why the triad of the Yeziratic Gevurah-Tiferet-Hesed is sometimes called the place where the angels stand guard over the Soul. Indeed this symbol takes on more meaning when one realizes that the upper face of Eden and the lower face of Heaven lie beyond.

According to Tradition, each person has a good and evil angel to watch over him. This has a particular meaning in Kabbalah, where the right and left pillars are occasionally called the Good and Evil sides. On the Tree the right side is expansive and the left contractive, the right growth, the left decay, and so on, so that a picture emerges of the left side always being constrictive, rigid and severe and the side of death. On its own, this pillar's quality would make a cruel and hard Universe, as the Talmud states in its story of the making of the World; but the Lord balances it with the right side of Mercy and harmonizes it by the central column of equilibrium. This prevents the left pillar from becoming excessive in its tendency to Form. However the principle of rigidity is there, and when out of balance becomes what is known as Evil: the 'Other Side', as it is called in Kabbalah.

Evil has a place in the Universe. It is not at all as most of us visualize it. For example, a cesspool is a highly unpleasant place, but it is absolutely necessary so that the organic waste material may decay back into its various elemental components before being recycled into the earth or organic nature. Evil can be the decaying remnants of an old situation. If it were preserved, then the whole Universe would soon be filled with waste matter on every level. It has to decompose in order to release the Force, Form and Consciousness locked up in its being. The process is called in Kabbalah the 'Pit' or Gehennah: the Valley of Hell. This type of evil moreover is quite different from that of the Demonic Forces and Forms outside the main organization of the Universe, other than Satan, who is in the employ of God as the tester of Man.

The angel who resides in Gevurah is the agent of Judgement. His task is to apply severity when needed, and to assert functional evil, or the contractive principle on the Soul. When a person behaves rightly, this angel acts in the passive and contained role of discrimination. However, if he commits a misdemeanour, the angel then switches into the active aspect of Gevurah and as an apparent devil or evil angel drives him on to commit more indiscretions, until the situation is so bad, and the Judgement so harsh, that the pillar of Mercy swings into action. He is then confronted with the decision to repent and return to equilibrium, or to go on further into the Other Side and face more chastisement or even destruction through the overbalancing of his

Tree. This constant balancing act is known as the attraction of the Yazar Tov and the Yazar Harah, the Good and Evil impulses. While the options are offered by Good and Evil, the choice is left to the man. This is why the emotional triad Gevurah-Tiferet-Hesed is considered to be that of morality.

The kind of morality spoken of at this level has little to do with the customs and practices taught in Yesod. These ego-rules vary greatly from community to community, so that while it is considered immoral in one society to kill for revenge, in another it is thought of as a moral duty. As for conventions in sexual matters, these vary according to period, climate and country. For example in the Bible Jacob not only had more than one wife, but kept concubines as well. These were the Yesodic customs of that time and age, and had little to do with real morality, that is, correct conduct at the level of the Soul.

The Triad of the Soul is the emotional aspect of man. It is a quite distinct level of being, between the natural lower face and the supernatural upper face of Yezirah. The Triad is composed of Gevurah, which is represented in the passive outer side of Emotion; Hesed, which functions through the active or inner aspect of Emotion; and Tiferet, which as the reconciling principle expresses itself through emotional consciousness. Together they make the emotional undertow in life, the mostly quiet, but far from still, deep process of individual growth. The terms outer and inner Emotion, like all sefirotic names, are totally inadequate, but they express its Form and Force aspect. Emotion here is quite different from the passion of the animal triad of Hod-Tiferet-Nezah, with its attraction and repulsion, excitement and exhaustion. Outer Emotion, for example, is concerned with the passive response of the heart, the feminine aspect of a person and his emotional receptivity, while inner Emotion is essentially the active, vital and deep masculine driving force within him. The effect of the latter may not always be perceived directly, except over a whole lifetime. Together with Tiferet, outer and inner Emotion generates, for example, in a relationship, love with discrimination and control with gentleness. These and the qualities of charity, compassion, equanimity and devotion make up with the truth and beauty of the Self, the nature of the Soul, the vehicle of Self-consciousness.

As will be perceived by its position on the Tree, the Soul Triad has a kind of independent field of action above and below the two faces of Yezirah which are bound by either the fixed laws that govern the natural man or the submission of the will to service of the Lord. This gives the Soul its power of choice, and is why the factor of morality is centred here. Morality is an emotional matter. It concerns good and bad conduct. A person once in Tiferet can no longer be excused, because he has risen above the Yesodic conventions of his society. Indeed he often has to break them in order to escape, as Abraham did when he questioned his father's belief in idols. This places him in a situation where he has to rely on his own insight, which is a quality of the Soul. For a man who lives in the lower face of Yezirah there is no insight, nor is there any morality. He will steal as long as he is not caught, bear false witness if it suits him and covet his neighbour's property. He will even murder if it is absolutely necessary. An honest glance at the history of natural mankind reveals that all these vices are rampant among not only individuals but whole nations in their dealings with each other. This is why the Ten Commandments were given to the Israelites who had just left Egypt. As ex-slaves and natural men they were still under the rulership of the lower Yeziratic face, despite the fact that they had entered the animal triad of Awakening Consciousness.

To be in contact with the Soul Triad is to possess a conscience. The word 'conscience' means 'with-knowledge', with the implication that one has reached a certain point in spiritual growth. One of the functions of the Ten Commandments was to create a way of conduct for a people – or person – who as yet had no conscience, but needed some guidance on their journey to the Promised Land.

The Ten Commandments, like all other Biblical disciplines, are based on the Sefirotic Tree. Each Commandment relates to a sefirah, so that every Law is based on a Divine principle. For example, the Tenth Commandment, 'Thou shalt not covet . . .', obviously related to Malkhut, the sefirah of materiality, while 'Thou shalt not bear false witness against thy neighbour' clearly applies to Yesod the ego. The Commandment 'Thou shalt do no murder', when placed in Tiferet, is full of meaning in relation to the Self and Truth; while the First, 'Thou shalt have no other gods before me', could be nowhere else but in Keter. The other Commandments, I leave the reader to contemplate.

Conscience is composed of Love, Truth and Fear. These are the attributes ascribed to Abraham, Jacob or Israel, and Isaac when they are placed on Hesed, Tiferet and Gevurah. These quite distinct characteristics describe the three different ways a man may relate his Soul to the Divine. While one may be related through Fear, through Love or through true Knowledge of the Lord, all three approaches should be

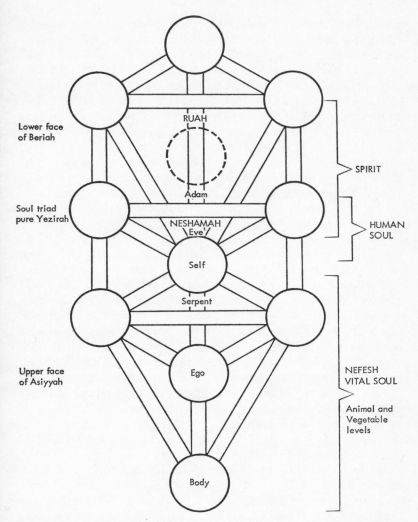

Lower face of Beriah

RUAH

Adam

Soul triad pure Yezirah

NESHAMAH

Eve

Self

Serpent

Upper face of Asiyyah

Ego

Body

SPIRIT

HUMAN SOUL

NEFESH VITAL SOUL

Animal and Vegetable levels

Figure 25. Souls. *In Kabbalah there are several levels of soul. The lowest is the vital soul of the natural body. Next is the Neshamah or human soul. This is defined by the triad Tiferet-Gevurah-Hesed and is therefore entirely Yeziratic. The triad Tiferet-Hokhmah-Binah contains the next level which is in Beriah. As part of the Realm of pure Spirit this soul is called the Ruah or the Spirit. Some Kabbalists reverse the names or use different arrangements but this is only a matter of titles.*

present in the Kabbalist; although he may have a preponderant incli-
nation towards one of them. This will bias the emotional loading of
his conscience, making him act (or refrain from acting) either because
he *fears* the Evil impulse or because he *loves* to do good. If he is working
primarily up the middle pillar he will want to do what is right because
he *knows* it conforms with the Heart of Hearts and the Will of God.
These three attitudes illustrate the three main methods by which a
person can approach God. All, it will be perceived, have to work
through the vehicle of the Soul.

In Kabbalah there are various levels of Soul. The first, as already mentioned, is the Nefesh or Vital Soul, that is the intelligence that inhabits
and governs the organic body and lower psyche. The next level is
that of the human Soul, as defined by the triad we have been examining. In the Zohar, the most widely read of Kabbalistic works, the
name 'Ruah' is used for the human Soul. However, not all Kabbalists
agree to this title: indeed in the Talmud the word is interchangeable
with Neshamah, which the Zohar regards as the higher Soul. To com-
plicate matters further, the great Rabbi Maimonides used the word
Nefesh for the most exalted level. In this and other books I have
returned to the Bible for a literary authority. In Genesis 1:2 the words
'*Ruah Elohim*' are used. They mean 'the Spirit of God'. Therefore I
have used the later term 'Neshamah' for the human Soul, the root
words being 'Neshemat Chyim', 'the breath of life' (Genesis 2:7), as
against Nefesh, the Vital Soul that animals possess, 'Nefesh Chyim',
'Living Creatures' (Genesis 1:20). In the Talmud a Neshamah has been
described as the particular disposition of a person, which, to my mind,
means the particular individuality of a human being. When set out on
the Tree of the psyche the Nefesh is in Asiyyah and the Ruah in Beriah,
with the Neshamah between in Yezirah (see Fig. 25).

The path letters that make up the Neshamah or Soul Triad spell out
the root word ZAKHEH, which underlies the terms 'purification' or
'to cleanse' and 'make bright'. This gives some idea of its function. It
is also called the Triad of Nourishment, in that there is a continuous
process of intake and refinement. In the physical body Tree of Asiyyah,
the same triad corresponds to the metabolism, where energy and
matter are broken down and built up, transformed and refined so that
the body's vitality is maintained at its maximum level. In the body
Tree (Fig. 9), the side functional triads of enzymes, hormones and
electrical ions adjoin the triad of metabolism and accelerate or retard
its level of vitality. So it is in the psyche, where the equivalent side

triads of emotional complexes and intellectual concepts stimulate or constrain the Soul. Here, in the depths of the Individual Unconscious, the active and passive emotional complexes and intellectual concepts of our lives influence our psychological metabolism. In natural man they remain the deep and largely unperceived promptings of the unconscious, but in one who is developing his Soul, the object is to transform these normally hidden operations into the experience of Self-consciousness. In this way the Soul is no longer an abstract symbol, something that most people suspect they possess, but becomes a living reality that is peculiarly one's own.

The individual Neshamah, Kabbalistic tradition says, is sent down into the World of Asiyyah in order to perform by virtue of its particular nature and talents, a specific task, which no other Soul can do. As an incarnate entity on earth, it is one of the highest levels of consciousness on the planet. Man, that is a full human being, is there not only to develop his Soul for himself, under difficult but highly stimulating conditions, but also as the sight, hearing, touch, smell and taste of the Lord at this level. As a Self-conscious Soul he remembers and is Remembered, knows and is Known. Because of this, the Lord perceives directly through human experience the World he has Called forth, Created, Formed and Made.

The human Soul of the Neshamah hovers above Asiyyah and below Beriah, and is usually referred to as female. It is sometimes seen as the Eve to the Spirit of Adam represented by the great Ruah Triad of Tiferet-Binah-Hokhmah. Below is the Serpent, or the Nefesh that bites Eve's heel as she presses on his head, where the Keter or Crown of Earth meets the Malkhut or Kingdom of Heaven in the sefirah of the Self. Here in the Self the threat of real temptation becomes present, and this is why the Soul must be purified before a Kabbalist can rise fully into the World of the Spirit.* This returns us to the question of Evil and one of its particular functions.

Of all the different forms of evil the most well known is the archetypal Devil of Satan. Traditionally Satan was once an archangel, that is one of the intelligences or guardians of the World of Creation. His task is to act as the Tempter, to test Truth and try out Goodness at the level of the Spirit. His brief is wide, in that he may lie and distort the appearance of reality so as to examine the flaws for discipline (Gevurah),

*For a detailed account of the Soul see the section 'The Soul' in the author's *Adam and the Kabbalistic Tribe*, Rider & Co., London, and Weiser, New York, 1974.

truth (Tiferet) and love (Hesed) of the Soul Triad. As one maggid remarked, 'All people are good when things are going well. But make difficulties for them and one soon observes who behaves well on principle and who for personal interest.' This on the human scale is the function of Satan, as the story of Job illustrates.

One day the Lord said of his servant Job, 'There is none like him in the earth, a perfect and an upright man, one that feareth God, and escheweth evil.' Because of this Job was awarded much wealth, children and a goodly life. But from among the Sons of God, Satan said that it was not difficult for Job to be all these things when he was so well placed and protected by God. Let Job be tried and he will curse God. Then the Lord, to demonstrate the quality of Job's soul, gave the Adversary leave to torment him by removing, at first all his family and wealth, and then his health, so that he was near to death. This follows the strict instruction that Evil cannot ultimately destroy good although it may press it hard. The test continued over many pages of dialogue between Job and his friends, who were convinced that he must have committed some misdemeanour to earn all his misery. Job denied this, even in the midst of his suffering: 'He knoweth the Way that I take: when he hath tried me, I shall come forth as gold.' The symbol of metal being burnt, purified, drossed and tempered is a very precise description of such proofings. Job was eventually given back all he had, indeed twice as much as before, as is often the case after a test of the Soul.

Job's viewpoint underlies the Kabbalistic philosophy that even the most corrupt Evil has within it a spark of Good that can be raised up and brought back into harmonious circulation. This daring approach, however, requires the rare purity of Soul found among saints and Zadekim who see evil performing a cosmic task as part of, and not separate from, God's Will.

The first conscious contact with Evil comes in the form of our own personal devil, who embodies the dark side of our ego. This sinister *alter ego* is a subtle fellow. He takes a long time to identify, but he must be identified before he can be dealt with. The maggid can help by pointing the villain out when he blows his cover and only the aspirant himself cannot see it. This attack on the personal devil is only one of several conversion exercises that take place on the lower half of the Yeziratic Tree. There is, for example a far more powerful devil that hovers about the Self. As the Keter of Asiyyah the Self is the physical glory of natural man, and as the Tiferet of Yezirah it takes the form of

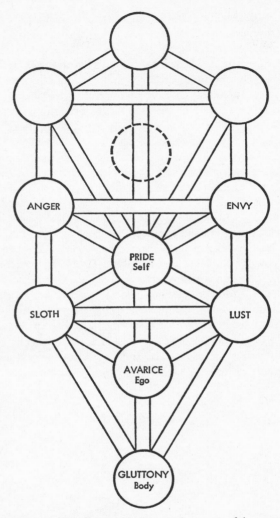

Figure 26. Seven Deadly Sins. *Each sin is the reverse of the normal operation of a sefirah. Its action prevents all adjacent triads and paths from working properly. As blocks on the Yeziratic Tree the Sins thwart the Kabbalist's progress from the dominance of Asiyyah, through the psyche and into the World of the Spirit or Beriah that lies beyond the seven lower sefirot.*

his psychological vanity. Both forms of Self-love block the entrance to Beriah, the world of Pure Spirit. They often merge into the Sin of Pride, which is one of the Seven Deadly Sins. These demonic attributes are the evil side of the Seven Lower Sefirot of Construction in the human psyche and body. Thus, for the physical sefirah of Malkhut, Sin is the unbalance and temptation of Gluttony; for Yesod, the ego's Avarice in its desire to claim everything; and for the swift and intelligent sefirah Hod the perversion is Sloth. Lust obviously relates to the instinctive and active Nezah, and Anger to an uncontrolled Gevurah, while Envy is clearly the opposite to the love and generosity of Hesed. Each of these Deadly Sins, as they are called, inhibits spiritual progress and has to be checked and converted by the work of the Soul, which has the power to purify.

The kind of Evil that hovers above the level of the Soul Triad and Lower Spirit is beyond the comprehension of most natural men; but perhaps a hint of higher temptation is gained by a moment in T. S. Eliot's play *Murder in the Cathedral*, where Thomas à Becket awaits his assassination. After a series of scenes in which the archbishop easily handles the worldly enticements, he is assailed very subtly from within by the attraction of dying a noble martyr. This is quite an unexpected and different order of testing, and is summed up in the lines 'The last temptation is the greatest treason: to do the right deed for the wrong reason.' Such a trial is placed before every Kabbalist, and is indeed always present at all levels on Jacob's Ladder.

25
Kavvanah: Intention

In order to enter the Kingdom of Heaven a man must rise through various stages. This means mastering the Natural World and embarking on the Work of the Chariot. The Chariot is the World of Yezirah, and so far we have reached up to the Triad of the Soul. According to Tradition some Kabbalists speak of *descending* in the Chariot; and this gives us an insight into two ways of regarding the Extended Tree of the Four Worlds. In order to rise up Jacob's Ladder of the Relative Universe one must descend into the depths of ones' own being. Here we see a simultaneous inner and outer movement, where the microcosm of Man reflects the macrocosm of the Manifest World. Because of this inter-relation, both the greater and the lesser affect each other. While man is obviously subject to the upper Worlds, the reverse is also true, although to a greatly lesser degree. A mundane example of this law is the phenomenon that occurs when a great liner is moored near to a small vessel. Such is the mutual attraction between the two boats that while the greater has a bigger effect on the smaller ship, it in turn will nevertheless exert a pull on the larger vessel. The same thing is observed in celestial bodies. A lesser planet may be more dramatically affected by a larger brother's presence, but the greater planet is, in proportion to the mutual mass relationship, in turn deflected, however slightly, from its orbit. So it is in the relationship between Man and the Universe. However, there are variable factors, because all men are not of the same spiritual weight.

At the lowest level we have vegetable man. He is almost totally passive. The Soul is present within him, but it is no more than a seed. He carries little or no weight spiritually, because he possesses no real will or capacity to even move outside the rhythms that keep him alive. Moreover he has no conscience, because his main concern is just with survival. His place in the world is as a seedbed for future generations. His well-being is taken care of by Nature, who is not concerned with individuals but large numbers. Any movement or ripple through the mass of humanity comes from above or below, like the wind over the surface of a lake or an earthquake beneath. Such a level of existence is neither good nor bad. It has its place as the sustainer of life, and as such is called in Kabbalah the 'Body' and the 'Flesh' level of consciousness. From the point of view of spiritual growth its power and substance can be converted from an inhibiting factor into a vital dynamic vehicle which will serve the supernatural part of man. This can only be done by someone who has cultivated his will. For without the control of will to focus physical action, the body soon grows tired and seeks rest, food and new excitement.

The training of the body is long and difficult, but it is possible to command it to an extraordinary degree, as several traditions demonstrate. Apart from the obvious discipline of Indian yoga, there are the whirling Dervishes of the Mevlevi Order, who spin on the axis of one toe for a duration of time long past the normal tolerance of giddiness. In Kabbalah there are various methods by which the will of the body is subdued and the power of conscious intention developed. To fast is one example, and to overcome sleep and remain alert by sheer will-power is another. These exercises, however, have to be closely supervised by people who know what they are doing. To do them without a specific reason is pointless and even dangerous.

The mastery of the animal part of the Nefesh is the next stage and level. Here again the will is applied, but this time to control the passions. This may mean learning how to sit absolutely still for an hour a day, or pressing even further the rebelling animal nature in some task it does not wish to fulfil. For example a man may be asked to perform a Kabbalistic task on the day he has some particularly pleasant social engagement. He may consider it unfair, but he will still have to decide whether or not he will do it. The animal part, deprived of its pleasure, will be annoyed; but the human part may see the purpose of the deliberately awkward timing. Such a test can often precipitate an all-out war by the Nefesh, aided by the ego against the maggid, the group and Kabbalah. However the real battle is within the man. If he is vitally interested in developing a Soul he will perceive and apply conscious intention. This is valuable experience and a part of his training and process of purification.

Assuming he has passed through these various stages of evolution and has reached the level where he can, at will, enter Tiferet, his position is very different from that of vegetable and animal man. As a being in conscious touch with three Worlds, he carries more weight to affect the Universe than perhaps a vast crowd-filled Olympic stadium. The reason for this is simply that, while he is in the state of Gadlut, the major condition, he is an instrument through which the upper World influxes may pass up or down. Of course the significance of the situation is not obvious to ordinary men, but history reveals the effects of this kind of power through the persons of such men as Jesus and the Buddha. Had these two not been at least at the place of the Self, neither would have had any real impact on the people about them, or on subsequent generations. Indeed, the power that came down through them may be judged by the fact that their influence is still present two thousand years or more later. No animal man's influence, however all-conquering, has lasted that long. The empires of Attila the Hun and Alexander the Great have vanished almost without trace, but the words of Plato and Zoroaster are still as fresh and powerful today.

The state of Devekut or communion with the Lord is a condition of passive affiliation. It requires not only being in Tiferet as often as possible, but a constant remembrance of His Presence. This is a preparatory situation for Grace to descend. There is, however, another state possible in Tiferet, and this is the active condition of Kavvanah. As will have been perceived much of the practical training of Kabbalah has been devoted to the development of will. We have now reached a point when the will is not only directed downward but upward with conscious intent. This is the meaning of Kavvanah.

It will be remembered that the animal triad of Awakening Consciousness is sometimes called the Triad of Hope, and that when Yesod and Tiferet are correctly aligned between Hod and Nezah, it becomes the Bow of Hope. In Kabbalah prayer is seen as a bow and arrow, with Kavvanah as the aim that a man takes, with the bow of his own being, up the central column of the Tree.

It is said of this act of spiritual archery that the man is in fact aiming himself, and that even before the arrow is loosened he must have become one with the target. In the arts of action, devotion and contemplation the analogy is borne out. In order to reach God one must be in as true an alignment up and down the pillar of Holiness as humanly possible. This requires great attention with minimal veering to the left or right pillars. It also needs one's feet firmly on Malkhut, one's ego mind clearly aimed in a passive Yesodic arrow and a disciplined hold of the bow of will in Tiferet. The shot may take the form of a ritual, a prayer or an idea. It does not matter. What is important is that the intention is right and conscious.

The rightness of such an operation is governed by the purity of the Soul Triad. Here the balance of Fear and Love of God corrects the emotional weighting of the act. There can be no entry of evil intent at such a moment, because the arrow would not only fall very short but penetrate the left-hand pillar and release whatever demonic forces were struck. This means in ordinary psychological terms, for example, an excess of zeal that could lead, and has done in the past, to religious persecution. The people who burnt heretics were all doing it for God, but in the impurity of their morality the arrow of their intention struck Gevurah and evoked the demonic archetype embodied in the Inquisition. This is why the Soul or level of Self-consciousness must be continually worked on, since to imagine one has reached absolute purity and perfection of Judgement and Mercy, is to commit blasphemy. It is a continuous process of emotional refinement, with Judgement and Mercy not only applied, by oneself, to matters below but also implemented upon one from above. The Soul, it is said, is that part of us that knows all about our particular life and everyone and everything connected with it. This makes it the vehicle through which we see the upper Worlds. The condition of such a subtle body determines the steadiness of our intentions and aim.

An act of worship without Kavvanah, Kabbalists say, is like a body without a Soul. Here is the difference between a man being spiritually asleep or awake. To recite our prayers without thought, because it is the socially accepted thing, or because that was the way one's parents taught one to do it, is never to rise above the level of Yesod, and therefore to have no contact with Heaven. Even to know the theory of Hod and the practice of Nezah is insufficient, because simply to repeat a formula without direct experience still confines one to the level of a clever vegetable. In the natural man there is, however, some possibility of religious experience in Tiferet: the Triad of Hope (Hod-Tiferet-Nezah) can awaken a moment of Self-consciousness, but this is subject to an excess of fervour, as the passion of the animal triad, with no conscious will in Tiferet, swings from elation to exhaustion, as Hod and Nezah oscillate without discipline. Such ecstatic moments are extremely moving to natural man, and spiritual teachers have to watch very carefully over their flocks and warn them of the dangers of unconscious ecstasy. 'The objective', one wrote, 'is to be moved without being moved.' To do this requires at least Self-consciousness, great will and much discipline.

The act of Kavvanah is one of conscious intention. It is accompanied by mastery over Malkhut the body, rulership over Yesod (so that the mind becomes a bridge and not a barrier) and the application of Hod's theory and Nezah's skill. When attention is focused in Tiferet, where the aim of the Kavvanah is governed, it is given emotional power and precision by the Hesed and Gevurah of the Soul. From the pivot of the Self, a man may raise the Spirit upwards to either praise or petition.

The act of Kavvanah can be directed to any level of the upper Worlds. Where will is there is power. Therefore what a man consciously intends may, if it is also Willed from above, come about. That is why a Kabbalist must be responsible to both Man and God.

26
Preparation

While the act of Kavvanah – conscious intention – is in Kabbalistic principle always the same, there are three methods by which it is applied. These relate directly to the approaches of Action, Devotion and Contemplation. However, before any of these methods can be implemented, preparations have to be made to lift the person out of the Katnut state of Yesodic consciousness.

The first and most practical preparation is that of external conditions. Traditionally one may perform the act of Kavvanah in public or private. The public approach has the advantage of the resources of a group. This comes in the form of a common purpose and mutual aid which can focus and raise the group's attention into a very powerful emotional state from which individuals can ascend even higher. This drawing on the soul of the group is common to all traditions, and may be seen in Quaker meetings, Buddhist meditation gatherings and Sufi zikres. In Kabbalah this may take place in open or closed groups. The open groups are not in fact open, because they are usually confined to very orthodox communities, like the Hasidim, where, although one may visit by permission, one may not be sufficiently familiar in that branch of the Tradition to become easily involved in the operation. Even within the Hasidic line there are quite different approaches to the same objective. One group will pray without any physical movement, while another will move about with extreme vigour, even the elders engaging in the dancing.

Of the closed groups less detail can obviously be given, because by their very nature very little is generally known of their methods. What can be said is that each group has its own way of doing things, even though the laws are the same, because, like people, groups have their own individual make-up and needs. There is no fixed format in the methods of Action, Devotion and Contemplation. Each age produces its own versions. The ritual of one period may well be redundant in the next, and any belief that the strict following of a literal formula is going to bring results, is an unperceptive miscalculation. The only thing that makes any of the methods work is Kavvanah – conscious intention.

The private approach is more difficult than the public, because there is not a conducive atmosphere generated by other people gathered in that place for that purpose. However, it does have the advantage that it can never degenerate into a social situation, such as can be observed in many synagogues and churches. On one's own, there can be no projection, no communal identification or external blame or praise. The success or failure of the operation is entirely in one's own hands.

The first task in the private situation is to create the internal conditions for rising from Katnut to Gadlut, and this, even in group work, is a necessary prerequisite, for one cannot rely on external stimuli to remind one of who one is, where one is and why one is there. This responsibility is one's own discipline. A maggid may set out rules, give instruction and provide devices and situations for wakening up, but he is not responsible for anything but his own work. Everyone, therefore, is his own taskmaster.

In order to aid the preparation a special time or place is usually devised by the maggid for the group, or by a man for himself. Many traditions use dawn and dusk as a time, and Kabbalistically this relates to the two pillars; the opening of the day's possibilities with Hesed, and the closing with the reflections and judgement of Gevurah. Indeed, in Judaic Kabbalah, it is said that Abraham instituted the morning and Isaac the evening prayer. As times change and we no longer live in a cycle governed by daylight, the two periods of action, devotion or contemplation may take place at the best time between dawn and noon, and between noon and dusk. Noon represents the middle column, and should be a third moment of daily Kavvanah.

The physical place where the conscious turning upwards and inwards occurs is preferably in a special space set aside for the purpose. It may be a simple room, or even a corner. It may also be a particular chair or carpet used exclusively for the operation. The principle is that that place or object is sanctified, if only in one's mind. This creates a condition of reminding one of the state required for Kavvanah. Over a long period the place will become charged because, if communion is constantly reached, that which is received will be imparted even to the Asiyyatic surroundings of a Kabbalist. The phenomenon of a place used for prayer having a praticularly dynamic or peaceful atmosphere is not uncommon. Many monasteries have it, and holy places throughout the world indicate that the descent of the upper Worlds into Asiyyah must have taken place there.

The combination of time and place, especially if set into a daily and weekly rhythm, help to bring the body and the psyche into a coordinated focus. The return of the Sabbath is the sefirah of Malkhut, the natural place of the Shekhinah or the Presence of God. On that day all the Worlds are in joyful union. The other six days may be seen as the six stages of spiritual progression through the week from Keter to Malkhut. On the basis of this concept some orthodox Kabbalists see each day of the week as a sefirotic quality and observe its work in their own conduct and attitudes. The elaborate celebration of the Sabbath as the Bride of Malkhut by the Lurian school of Kabbalists is a historical example of this.

For people who live under twentieth-century conditions it is a question of adapting the rhythm to their own time-scale. The recognition of the necessity for half an hour's meditation in the morning and evening at a certain time reinforces the passive state of Devekut or constant remembrance, as well as the active practice of Kavvanah. Of course sometimes it is not always possible to be in the place especially designed for the purpose, but here the miraculous in Kabbalah enters, because in a split second of remembrance on seeing the clock stand at noon, while walking down a street or in the middle of work, one can be moved from the petty concerns of the Yesodic ego into the still centre of the Self, where three Worlds meet in the Presence of the Lord. This experience is sometimes more deep than one obtained during a Sabbath-day meditation.

The next step is to prepare oneself. This begins with the body. The very orthodox, before they begin the act of Kavvanah, bathe and

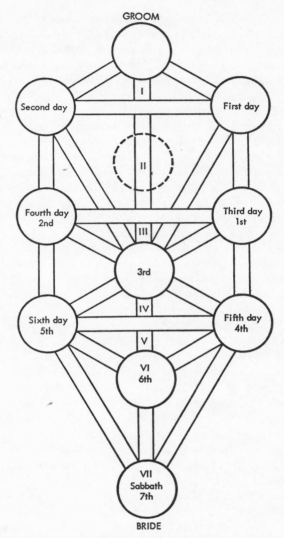

GROOM

Second day

First day

I

II

Fourth day
2nd

Third day
1st

III

3rd

Sixth day
5th

IV

Fifth day
4th

V

VI
6th

VII
Sabbath
7th

BRIDE

Figure 27. Holy Week. *Here are three ways in which Creation was manifested. The first system sets out the days on the functional pillars of the octave, while the second corresponds only to the seven lowest sefirot of Construction. The third takes the seven days to be the central triads descending into the last two sefirot, with Adam being created as the image in Yesod on the sixth day. All the systems are valid. The Sabbath is traditionally known as the Bride who awaits the Groom of Keter: the beginning and end.*

evacuate their bowels. Besides the obvious elimination of physical discomfort and therefore of bodily distractions during the operation, the practice of ablution informs the Nefesh of what is about to happen. This is important because the body has an intelligence of its own, and, with the help of training and consciousness, will aid the person to obtain the best conditions for Kavvanah. To enlist this help involves one in taking care of the body so that it does not set its considerable will against one's Tiferet and so create conflict. Fasting or indeed any bodily torment is neither required nor of any merit if it is done for its own sake. The body must be in such a state of equilibrium that it begins to be no more than a pleasant presence in the consciousness. It must never vanish from sight, for that would eliminate the Yeziratic Malkhut and make the Tree of the psyche incomplete and disconnected with Asiyyah. This would render Kavannah useless, because the influx from the upper Worlds could never reach Earth.

The second stage is to make the animal part of the Nefesh receptive. It is helped by having conducive surroundings; such as neutral colours, objects that create inner and outer quiet, or views that soothe the desires and reactions of the flesh. Although music and dancing may arouse the Triad of Awakening Consciousness, these stimulants have to be applied under great discipline, so that the person does not, as sometimes happens, fall into a state of uncontrolled exaltation in which Tiferet consciousness is lost amid the excitement of Yesodic ecstasy. This condition is strictly warned against in Kabbalah, where one never surrenders oneself except to God. The excitement that is generated by some branches of every tradition is not so much Self-consciousness as the Self-unconsciousness of possession by the animal triad. That is why, unless one is under a strict discipline, the passions of the animal triad should not be aroused. One cannot enter the Kingdom of Heaven with the bit between the teeth. It is better to ride in on a short rein and in total control.

The third stage is to clear the mind of the Yesodic ego. This is accomplished by either concentration or radiation. The first technique is to concentrate on an action, a prayer or an idea, depending on which of the three methods one is to follow. This will focus the attention and bring the theory of Hod and the practice of Nezah into relation with Malkhut below and Tiferet above. The technique of radiation is the reverse, in that one dwells on nothing: that is, the consciousness ignores all the thoughts, feelings and images that pass before the mind's eye on the Yesodic screen. For a while the ego will try to intrude, but it will

Figure 28. Tetragrammaton.   *The Name given by God to Moses has been used in many ways by Kabbalists. Here the letters Yod–Heh–Vav–Heh have been arranged to form the figure of a man. This is Adam in the likeness of his Maker.*

then withdraw, slowly and become quiescent, until energy is drawn away from its preoccupations and it has to join in the sefirotic combination that is building up throughout the lower face of Yezirah. When either technique is properly carried out over a long period, the body, Nefesh and ego eventually respond, if only out of habit. This makes the initial part of the operation easy, because all the organic forces start to accept and then work for one.

At the point when there is sufficient inner equilibrium of body and ego mind, the evocation to begin can be started. All Kabbalistic evocations are based on the Tree, because they are designed actually to raise one up through the Worlds. Let us take one of the most simple examples, where a man stands up to commence the operation. The action of standing is not just a formal mark of respect, but a manifestation of the approach of Action, in that a man uses his body. This physical vehicle is the Asiyyatic image of his maker, based on the design of the Tetragrammaton, the most widely known Kabbalistic name of God, made up of the four Hebrew letters Yod-Heh-Vav-Heh. Some Kabbalists arrange the name vertically, as shown in fig. 28, to show that the figure of a man, Adam, is to be seen. This, like the Sefirotic Tree, has four levels within it, each letter representing one of the Four Worlds, so that as a Kabbalist stands up to begin his evocation, his body becomes a physical reminder that he is an image, a likeness of all Manifest Reality in miniature. The ritual is carried further when he raises his arms so as to bring the two outer pillars of his hands, at Hod and Nezah, up through the Gevurah and Hesed and into the Binah and Hokmah position. With his feet firmly planted on the ground his body forms the central column. He then speaks the words:

'LORD THOU ART GOD'

This again is no simple evocation. It is a precise raising of the consciousness up the Tree of the man. 'Lord' or ADONAI is the God Name for Malkhut, and 'Thou' is associated with Tiferet, while 'God' is the English term used for Keter. Here we have the conscious connecting of the Yeziratic Malkhut, which as the Asiyyatic Tiferet is the central nervous system, up through the ego to the Self and then beyond to the Keter of Yezirah. This Keter is the simultaneous Tiferet of Beriah, the World of the Throne and the Malkhut of Azilut, the World of the Glory. The Malkhut of Azilut is the Divine ADONAI that is reflected in the Malkhuts of all the lower Worlds. It is also the place of the Shekhinah, so that a man who is aware during this moment of action, devotion and contemplation, not only makes a union between all his physical, emotional and intellectual faculties, but joins, in his being, all the Worlds above and below.

In such a moment the man will be drawn up into the Daat of his incarnate psyche, which is also the Yesod of the Spirit, there to meet the descent of the Presence. In the utter silence and stillness of the next stage of Devekut communion he will face his unseen Maker. On his return from the level of the Second Heaven the Kabbalist completes the evocation with the words:

'THE LORD IS IN HIS TEMPLE.
LET ALL THE WORLD KEEP SILENT BEFORE HIM.'

27
The Approach of Action

All three Approaches, whether they be Action, Devotion or Contemplation, are precisely what they say – approaches. Moreover, although the techniques may differ widely according to time, place and custom their objective is the same: that is to reach at least the state of Gadlut, if not to penetrate deep into the upper Worlds.

The Approach of Action has for obvious reasons great appeal and application to those people who like to do things, be active and physically involved in an operation. This is because their type is focused in the Malkhut-Yesod-Nezah triad. Such a physical outlook, it must be repeated, is in no way inferior to those of feeling and thinking, because these other two tendencies are also confined to the great lower triad of Hod-Malkhut-Nezah, which belongs to the Katnut or minor state. For example, although a man may possess a vast amount of Hodian learning about Kabbalah he may be just as egocentric as the feeler, or the doer, because they all centre on Yesod, the ordinary level of ego consciousness.

This gives us an insight into why the three Approaches exist. Like a cold petrol engine, the psyche has to be initially turned over by a starter, such as the ritual of evocation described in the last chapter, before it can begin to fire off its own systems. Once running, the mental mechanism begins to tune and the psychological vehicle warms up. The purpose of the three Approaches is to get one particular subtriad of the lower face of the Yeziratic Tree going well. With this accomplished, the Tiferet connection made during the evocation can then flow down through that triad's path and so activate the others. When the whole of the lower face is ready, the vehicle, or Chariot, to use the traditional term, is ready to go where it is directed.

One of the most simple techniques of Action is the breathing meditation. Many traditions use this natural cycle, and Kabbalah is no exception. Here the Tetragramaton, pronounced YAHVEH, is spoken silently, its two syllables divided between the inward and outward breath, so that Yah flows with inhalation and Veh with the exhalation. The process may also be reversed. The aim is not mechanically to repeat God's Name, but to be constantly mindful of Him through the moment-by-moment rhythm of breathing, also to remember how he breathed life into Man and made him a Neshamah, a living, breathing Soul. The result should be a frequent state of Gadlut no matter where we are, or what we are doing. To realize that one's existence depends on breath, and to accompany the realization with the personal Name of God, is to raise the consciousness, if only for a few seconds every minute, and to spin a thread of Devekut for the Soul.

Another simple physical technique is the walking prayer or meditation. Here the action of stepping off the right and then the left foot can be used to bring the two side pillars of the Sefirotic Tree into consciousness. With the column of Mercy on the right and Severity on the left, any short or long walk, wherever one is going, can be transformed into an act of devotion and contemplation. This is accomplished by constantly remembering that the trunk of the body is the middle pillar. With a certain amount of practice there will soon be two levels of consciousness present. The Yesodic to make sure one does not get run over or walk into a lamp post, and the Tiferet which observes both above and below, the inner and the outer Worlds. In such a condition illumination can come. A man walking down a busy street can quite suddenly join the outer and the inner Worlds in a union of upper and lower faces of the Yeziratic Tree. This brings both the upper face of Asiyyah and the lower face of Beriah into contact through the unification of three Worlds in the Self. In such a moment, Heaven and Earth meet, and the street is converted into Paradise, although perhaps only the meditator can perceive it.

In addition to this walking technique is the application of the God Names associated with each pillar. YAHVEH is said to be the merciful side of God, while ELOHIM is the severe or just aspect. If the first Name is silently spoken on the right step and the second on the left, and there is maintained, above and between, the God Name EHYEH, I AM, then again the state of a Gadlut and Devekut cannot but occur. Such methods may appear to be simple, but they are not easy, because to maintain the discipline constantly and regularly requires a great effort of will. To repeat them mechanically is not only worthless but taking the Lord's Name in vain, that is, without being mindful of Him. Therefore one does not begin such exercises unless one's intention is correct.

Ritual is an important aspect of the Approach of Action. The reason for this is that it must be carried out with great precision, and this requires a special attention. The most common form of ritual is the religious service. These vary, even within the Jewish Tradition. For example, there is a distinct difference between the Askenazi or northern Jewish ritual and the Sephardi or southern and oriental rites. These differences are not important; what is important is that they are carried out correctly and with Kavvanah. To perform the most elaborate ritual in a state of Katnut invalidates its purpose, whereas a man who recites a single God Name fully aware of why he is doing it may achieve not only Gadlut, but union with the Divine. The Lord is concerned with quality, not quantity.

In ancient Israel the rituals in the Temple were complex as well as profound. They required maximum attention and eye for detail. This still applies to the techniques of ritual, no matter what branch of the Kabbalistic Tradition one may belong to. The whole essence of ritual, I repeat, is not the format, although this may be loaded with meaning, but the careful observation and discipline that are maintained while performing it. In Freemasonry, a European offshoot of Kabbalah, a man may have to spend years taking part in a ceremony before he is allowed to conduct it. Moreover, no one will teach him directly how to do it. He has to watch, observe and absorb every tiny detail of the procedure so that it becomes second nature. When his turn comes, he can then go through all the motions with infinite precision, while his attention is concerned with the real object of the whole exercise. If the Lodge is a living one, he may draw on the mutual soul of its members and so join them all in the experience. This principle applies to all group ritual work.

A ritual is a kind of miracle play, in which the state of Man and his relationship to the World and God are set out in semi-dramatic form. Usually it also describes, in allegorical action, Man's ascent, tests and accomplishment in spiritual evolution and union with the Godhead. Most ritual ceremonies are concerned with the whole, or aspects, of this matter; although in some cases, because the real meaning is lost, the ceremony is no more than a lifeless shell. In Kabbalah there are many types of ritual, and every school or group has its own. We can still see, for example, some of the rituals of the Hasidim in present-day Jerusalem and read about the ceremonies of Greeting the Bride of the Sabbath by the Lurianic brotherhood in old Sefad. While these may be perfect in their own way, there is no absolute formula. Ritual is simply a method by which the person or persons physically create a situation which represents events or principles in or of the higher Worlds.

This is clearly set out in the ritual process followed by Dervish Turners, who spin up through the states of stone, vegetable, animal and man into union with the One. It may also be seen in the ritual of the Christian Easter, and in the domestic service of the Jewish Passover, whose symbolic dishes and discourse describe the going out of Egypt. To many, these ceremonies are no more than formal celebrations, but to those who have some insight and commitment to spiritual development, the unfolding rites are full of significance and have a power to raise the Soul above the patterned movements, words and music.

As regards Kabbalah, this book is not going to describe any Kabbalistic ritual in detail. One should not learn ritual through a book, because it takes the impact away when confronted by the reality. Moreover, ritual is basically a physical activity and should be taught directly by a maggid who knows one's individual requirements. Some people, for instance, need a ritual that demands an active Nezah role, so that their Hod receptivity is encouraged. This may mean that they stand absolutely still throughout a ceremony on full alert, or move and mime vigorously in tune with subtle inflections of word and music. To describe a ceremony in full would be even more misleading than to see it as a pure spectator, because all that would be revealed would be the literal form. This is why only general principles have been spoken of. One must be part of a ritual in order really to experience its nature and purpose.

Music and words play an important part in the Approach of Action, although superficially they appear to belong to the heart and head. Music, for example, is used in singing or chanting. The function of melody in this case, is to awaken Nezah's love of rhythm and mount its power. When a hymn is sung, it charges the words with the active principle and enlivens the body by making it wish to sway or dance. Music stimulates the Nezah-Yesod-Malkhut triad and creates, in a communal situation, a common theme for all to join in harmony, thus adding to the choir of focused energy. This focusing of attention rides on the fixed rail of the melody as it progresses, and guides the state of the group in a series of liturgical and musical steps towards the elated condition of Gadlut. It is possible, of course, for the reverse to happen, in that the physical excitement induced by the music and movement can create a purely Yesodic mood, as in a dance hall. Here the quality of the maggid or leader conducting the ceremony is revealed, for he has to control and direct the attention to the highest point of realization the group can communally reach, before they move into an individual and universal relationship with their Maker. This is as far as ordinary assembly work can go.

The method of music and dancing is not used as widely in Kabbalah as it is in other Traditions. It does not have a repertoire of sacred dances, such as those found in the East, although the orthodox branch does possess ancient ceremonies, liturgies and melodies. An example is the prayer of the Kaddish, dating back to the Temple, which is formally recited while standing and swaying in the synagogne, study house and by the grave. This ritual prayer, which is used as much as the Shema, is sung in praise of God at great speed, but with strict attention, by people who, although they do not understand its language word for word, know its implication. Here is an example of the technique of physical and spoken ritual transcending its action – providing it is done with Kavvanah.

Words in Kabbalah, as we have seen through the science of Gematria and the other letter and number studies, have great significance. The Bible, for instance, may be read in a variety of ways, such as connections seen through numerical equations, or differing versions of the Names of God. From the point of view of the Approach of Action, words and letters have been adopted as a method of inner ritual, so that a man may perform, in his mind, an exercise of manipulations as complex as any dance or song. We have already had two such exercises in the breathing and walking meditations which do not initially require anything more than to go through the action with conscious intention. In the case of the manipulation of the Hebrew Alphabet, Kabbalah has developed a special technique.

The Hebrew letters, it will be remembered, define the path relationships between the sefirot. In this manner they help to bring the Universe into being. This profound idea caught the imagination of some
Kabbalists, who sought to study the letters, their shapes and root
meanings by turning them over and over in their minds. Initially this
was a method of contemplation, but later it was developed into a
meditation technique in its own right, with definite benefits to even
the least intellectual of men – and there are non-intellectual Kabbalists.
Abulafia, a Kabbalist of the thirteenth century, was particularly interested in this method, and wrote much on it. He developed the idea of
moving the letters of the alphabet about, part in random and part by
inspiration, so as to gain a glimpse, through prophetic vision or deep
psychological insight; into the upper Worlds. Later Kabbalists took
the idea further, and a whole range of methods were formulated in
which the letters were used to induce the state of Gadlut. One technique, for example, was the passing of the letters before one's Yesodic
mind's eye, another of writing them down, so as to make up endless
chains of letters. Occasionally some combinations would make words.
These might or might not make sense. If they did, they could reveal
what was really in one's mind and therefore distracting the meditation
away from God. Or they could be hints or clues about the next
World. When the technique was applied to the Approach of Action,
the Kabbalist merely concentrated on the continuous interchanging of
the letter combinations, so that in the sheer lack of meaning all worldly
images, feelings and thoughts lost their form and one entered a realm
where there was nothing but a stream of letters that eventually dissolved into nothingness. This No-Thingness is what the Kabbalist
sought, for it took him into the Daat of Yezirah where he met the
Ruah Hakodesh – the Holy Spirit. Known as the Atomization of
Letters, this technique enabled the Kabbalist to attain Devekut by
swamping his Yesod with material totally incomprehensible to his
natural, sense-based Foundation, thus making it lose its power of per-
suasion over his attention, which could then be drawn upwards to
beyond the Self.

The principle described above equally applies to most meditation
techniques, where the person focuses upon a God Name. This has
already been touched on, in that the Name is held in the non-luminous
mirror of Yesod, reverberated by Hod and repeated by Nezah until
its form and sound, on being raised up to Tiferet, is dissolved with the
Self, in the union of Keter and Tiferet in Daat. In such moments

G

everything vanishes – body, Name and Self – to become one with the unknown and known.

The object of all these actions, be they simple or complex, active or passive, is to move out of the Katnut state and into the Gadlut; then on from the first stage of Devekut in Tiferet to the second in the Daat of Yezirah, the Yesod of the next World. To obtain this level in the Third Garden is quite possible by dozens of other physical devices, ranging from fasting at the ascetic end of the spectrum to the act of physical love at the other. For Kabbalists the whole of life is a ritual, each moment an act of conscious attention whether at work, play, prayer or study. Everything the Kabbalist does should be an act of worship. That is why the aspirant in the story came not to listen to his Zadek but to observe how he tied up his shoelace. In this practice is the essence of the Approach of Action.

28
The Approach of Devotion

The Approach of Devotion begins with the triad Hod-Yesod-Nezah. After the initial starter of an invocation that connects Yesod to Tiferet, prayer, meditation or whatever devotional technique is to be used, can be employed. These, like those of Action, vary over a wide range.

The most common form of devotion is the prayer. Let us begin with the most simple application. One may recite a prayer mechanically, that is, repeat it without any idea or feeling of what it is about. Such a phenomenon is commonplace in the formal religious services found in most churches, mosques and synagogues, because the vast majority of people do not know how to pray. To be able to pray means at least to acknowledge there is a state of Katnut and Gadlut, but few realize their condition and therefore cannot begin to pass beyond the repetition of meaningless words and over-worn phrases that most of their ancestors also used without comprehension. Without the connection between Yesod and Tiferet nothing can rise up or flow down. The story of Cain and Abel illustrates this theme. Cain's offerings remained below, and so he murdered his brother and still continues to do so to this day. As Genesis has Cain say: 'From Thy face shall I be hid; and I shall be a fugitive and a vagabond in the earth.' This is natural man's condition.

For the person who has knowingly experienced Gadlut, the situation is not the same. If he prays with the intention of rising up from the ego to the Self, his prayers take on a quite different character. First, he acknowledges that he is not the centre of his universe – which, alas, most people think they are, despite their noble protests. Second, he is prepared to submit to whatever he considers to be a manifestation of God, be it Buddha, Christ or the unseen Almighty. This makes him say his prayer with a distinct sense of direction, either to rise up to Heaven, or penetrate deep within his being, which, as we have noted, is the same thing. Such a presupposition is the beginning of Kavvanah, even for the untrained.

If we look at the position of the Hod-Yesod-Nezah triad on the Tree, we will observe that it is by nature introverted, that is inturning. It also overlays the Zadek path between Yesod and Tiferet, so that it has some involvement with the act of willingness, the first conscious step in the 'my will' and 'Thy Will' stages of development. This gives the devotional approach certain advantages over the methods of Action and Contemplation, in that it cuts to the minimum the distractions of the outer world, because, unlike the two outer triads, it has no direct contact with Malkhut. This is why the devotional type is to be found in great numbers in monasteries and closed communities. However it does also have its disadvantages, in that there is sometimes a naivety about ordinary life which can become, in an impure state, a hatred for worldly things. In Kabbalah this is not allowed to happen, because of the rule that Keter must reach Malkhut, otherwise the operation is incomplete. It is for this reason that Kabbalists marry, practise business and enjoy the pleasures of natural men. However, it is always done with the proviso that they constantly remember Heaven, so that Malkhut is connected with Keter and the Lightning Flash can flow through all the Worlds.

The man praying from the Hod-Yesod-Nezah triad cannot but pray with feeling. Thus, while he may say the prayer in a language alien to his normal speech, such as Hebrew, Aramaic or Latin, he will still sense the feeling of what he is saying. This is why, even amongst the illiterate who have learnt their prayers by rote, the presence of the Shekhinah, the Holy Spirit, is to be found.

While a prayer is basically an act of devotion, it may be performed in several ways and levels. For example, there is the way just mentioned, where a man repeats a prayer whose words he may not even understand. This need not matter, providing his intention is one of worship. In such a case the prayer becomes a poem of pure sound which is transformed into one long expressive word of significance to both the supplicant and to God. This, we are told, is quite acceptable to our Maker, who is concerned more with sincerity than linguistic ability.

The second form of simple prayer is when a man does understand what he is saying. Here the simple meaning of the words are dwelt on, so that the sense of the prayer is clearly seen and chosen for a particular kind of devotion. For instance, one prayer is designed as a thanksgiving grace before a meal, whereas another is only used at the deathbed, where a man wants an easy release from his Asiyyatic body. In the Jewish tradition there are indeed prayers for almost everything, including 'On hearing thunder'. This gives some idea how the state of Devekut or remembrance of God is maintained even in the most earthly of circumstance.

The understanding of the plain meaning of a prayer is taken yet further in devotional practice, in that every word is considered in its full implication. For an illustration take the Jewish prayer for bread, which runs: 'Blessed art thou, O Lord our God, King of the Universe, who bringest forth bread from the earth.' The first word, 'Blessed', is considered by two questions: What is to be blessed, and what does it mean to be blessed? The thoughts and feelings generated by these questions involve Grace, Providence, the descent of Will and a dozen other heavenly topics. Then the next word, 'art', the verb 'to be', has a vast Kabbalistic literature devoted to it and to the question of Existence. This is followed by the direct and personal 'Thou', whose implication is profound to the man praying, in that it is the selfsame 'Thou' which is immanent in him at the Tiferet of his Soul. The title 'Lord' prefixed by 'O' reveals, after the intimacy of the immanent 'Thou', the majesty of the Divine and the remoteness of the Transcendant Absolute En Sof 'Who' in the next phrase is related to as 'Our God'. In this is the whole Scheme of the Four Worlds. The title 'King of the Universe' opens out the worshipper's vision to appreciate the Governor of the workings of Providence, that is, all the interconnected Trees stretching between the highest Keter and the lowest Malkhut. It is this provider 'Who', the prayer goes on to say, 'bringest forth': a phrase which is rich in miraculous meaning and philosophical weight. And all this is the preface to the appreciation of 'bread', a highly charged symbol of the sustainer of life which comes 'from the earth', the seedbed of the Manifest Universe. No one who proceeds through a prayer in this way could fail to be moved. In it is contained the Absolute, his Will, his Unmanifest Existence, his Manifest Existence, and Providence, for man, that he may eat and live. No one could but be thankful for his daily bread when he considers how it came to be on the table before him.

Besides the plain meaning of the words in a prayer there is also their inner meaning. This may be applied in several ways, one of which is to regard each word as a Name of God. This concept derives from the notion that the whole of the Bible is composed of the titles of God. The origin of the idea is that, when the five books of Moses were first written down, there were no spaces between the words, so that by dividing the text up in various ways different meanings could be read into the text. This was considered valid by some Kabbalists, because all the letters, like the paths of the Tree, were expressions of the aspects of God. Therefore it did not matter how one read them, they were always versions of the single divine Name that stretched from the first letter in Genesis to the last in Deuteronomy. From the view of practical application, the devotee considered his prayer as a chanting of the Names of God. He might or might not know, by means of the science of numbers and letters, which Names, but this did not concern him, providing he was aware that he was passing them through his consciousness. Knowledge does not necessarily mean information. A man knows when he is in love. He does not need a psychologist's report on his symptoms or an X-ray of his heart to prove it.

Another application of the Hebrew letters in the devotional approach is to consider each word of a prayer as containing all the Worlds, all the Souls therein and the Presence of the Divinity throughout. As the Hebrew letters are the connections between the sefirot, making twenty-two principles that hold the Universe together, such a consideration in mind would make each word become a special combination of paths and meanings, which that word, in particular expressed. We have glimpsed a little of this in our analysis of the plain meaning of the words. Therefore if the word is dwelt on as an act of devotion in the Self there will occur a joining of the letters of the word in a human and Divine unity at the Lower meeting place of the Three Worlds. This brings about an ascent of 'immeasurable joy and delight', wrote one Hasidic Kabbalist. The objective eventually is to follow the words back to their source in the World of Azilut, and even pass beyond this Eternal realm into No-Thingness.

For obvious reasons the method of Allegory has a direct application to the Approach of Devotion. In this the Psalms and the Song of Solomon are prime examples. The Psalms were composed not only as religious poems but as the basis of liturgical hymns to be sung in the Temple. Poetry and music are both highly evocative arts which can transform the mood and atmosphere of a meeting in moments. They can be used with great effectiveness in an act of devotion, providing there is no ego element in the performance. As one maggid said to a musician at a ritual, 'If you play for your own glory and not God's, you have no place here.' The use of music to focus the attention and use it as a guide rail to ascend from Yesod to Tiferet has already been touched on. In the same way poetry can be applied to change the emotional state of an individual or group. In this case, it is not just the rhythms, textures and dramatic sounds and silences that aid the ascent, but the imagery invoked. Let us look at the example of the twenty-third Psalm.

In this evocation David perceives the Lord as his shepherd, a highly emotive role as the keeper and watcher over his Soul. He goes on, 'I shall not want.' This is an affirmation and submission to the Lord's protection. It speaks of a mutual love. It continues, 'He maketh me to lie down in green pastures (Asiyyah). He leadeth me beside the still waters (Yezirah).' Both these pastoral images create an emotional state of confidence, as do the next verses, with their symbols of walking safely through 'the valley of the shadow of death' (natural life) and being comforted by 'thy rod and thy staff' (Tradition and Revelation). The Psalm concludes with the allegory of a prepared table (Soul), the head (Spirit) anointed with oil (Grace imparted), and a cup running over (Grace received), finishing with the verse: 'Surely goodness and mercy shall follow me all the days of my life: and I will dwell in the house of the Lord for ever.' Imagine these lines spoken or sung to music in an atmosphere where a congregation was in the state of Gadlut. The effect would be to raise one's level high above the Mundane ego to that place where one no longer believed but *knew*, for certain, what was being sung about. In terms of the Tree one would have been lifted from the awakening Triad of Hope through the emotional Triad of Love and Charity and into the great Triad of the Spirit: the state of Faith and Knowledge.

The use of allegory to define the condition of devotional love is seen in the Song of Solomon. Here the Soul waits for the coming of the Spirit, or Eve for her Adam in the likeness of a man. The poem describes, in sensual form, the yearning of the Lover for the Beloved.

'By night on my bed I sought him whom my soul loveth: I sought him but I found him not.' That is, 'at night', or in spiritual sleep, 'on my bed' or while in the state of Katnut and Yesodic dreams, 'I sought him whom my soul loveth: but I found him not.' How could she? There is no Yesod-Tiferet connection in spiritual sleep. Nor is there when she wanders about the paths of the lower Yeziratic face, called in the Song 'the streets' of the city, even though she has, as the Song states, 'risen'. Shortly after, however, the watchmen or Tiferet finds her, she in turn finds him whom she loves. 'I held him, and would not let him go, until I had brought him into my mother's house, and into the chamber of her that conceived me.' That is, the Soul brought the Spirit into Yesod and then down to Malkhut, sometimes called the lower Mother. Here the Bridegroom of Keter is brought into contact with the Bride of Malkhut.

The apparently sensual language in which the Song continues is designed to change the state of both singer and listener. The erotic theme, as a method of presentation of ideas appears throughout the development of Kabbalah, so that the union between Soul and Spirit is allegorically expressed in the sexual act. This often misunderstood mythology of sensuality is used because, for many people, the act of love is the high peak of their physical and emotional lives. To use the power of the most natural and potent of mankind's experiences is considered so legitimate that the relationship between Moses and the Shekhinah is described in the Zohar in terms that many conventional and literal-minded rabbis have never been able to accept.

The symbol of the Lover and the Beloved describes very well the essence of the Approach of Devotion, even to the point that the Lover also fears his or her Beloved. In Mundane life the lover is fearful of offending the beloved; but the relationship between the devotee and his Lord involves a different form of fear. A man may pray because he loves God; he may also pray because he fears him. This is quite an acceptable act of devotion in Kabbalah, because 'To fear the Lord is the beginning of Wisdom'. While according to some Kabbalists this is a less desirable approach to God, at least it does mean an emotional, or Soul Triad awareness of his Presence, as against the nominal recognition by one who lives in the egocentric universe of Yesod. A man who fears God has the beginnings of a developing Soul. He will act devotedly through Gevurah, to live by the way of Justice on the Form column. On the other hand, a true Hasid, who loves God, will live by Hesed and the way of Righteousness. While the one will be correct in refraining from evil and the other live piously by performing good acts, the Kabbalist endeavours to live by balancing the active and passive approaches on the central column of consciousness and Know-ledge – the Way of Holiness. A man who is devoted to this middle Way both fears and loves his Lord. He also yearns continually for his Presence. All his actions, both above and below, within and without, are devoted to God. He seeks his Beloved everywhere, sometimes even forgetting himself.

The losing of the Self is a phenomenon of spiritual work, and there are two attitudes to it within the Kabbalistic Tradition. Some Kabba-lists work on forgetting oneself, so that the union with their Lord is in no way impaired, while others maintain that a man must retain his consciousness to the very last moment, before complete union, because while a man is still incarnate on the earth his task is to help bring down the influx of Grace to the lower Worlds. To go up out of Manifest Existence before one's task is done could be a supreme act of selfishness. My own conclusion is that when one is ready to go, like Enoch who walked with God, one will be taken and no longer be separated from Him. The time and place is the choosing of the Beloved.

29
The Approach of Contemplation

Within the Judaic tradition study is considered as a form of contemplative prayer. Indeed so strong is this idea, that if there was the choice of pulling down the study house or the village synagogue, the preference was always to preserve the study house. Moreover, the rabbinical ruling went on to state that a synagogue could be converted into a study house, but not the reverse. All this indicates a deep respect for the Contemplative Approach.

The initial act of contemplation begins with the Hod-Yesod-Malkhut triad of Yezirah. Here the ego examines, in a reflective manner, the information of Hod in the logic of Malkhut. This is why there are so many rabbinical commentaries on the Bible, and indeed in Kabbalah, that follow set forms of thinking. The sciences of numerology and letters originate in this triad; however, if they are not transcended they can keep the mind of the aspirant still entrapped within the great ego-centred triad of Malkhut-Hod-Nezah or the Katnut condition. Here is the reason for the warning that such studies can lead to a dead end, because being primarily on the passive side there is no impetus to escape the fascinating world of word and number. The techniques of Gematria and Notarikon are means, not ends.

Let us begin with an example of contemplation in an area we have already touched upon. As we have seen, the letters of the Hebrew alphabet have more significance than merely being the components of words. They also have greater scope than the numerical values placed on them, because they were incorporated into the Kabbalistic scheme of the Universe to express certain sets of laws. For instance, the letters Shin, Mem and Aleph were called the three mother letters of the World, because they represented the active, passive and neutral principles that govern, create form and make Manifest Existence. Their six possible combinations determine the quality of a given situation, making it a growing one in this case, or a decaying one in that. For the contemplative the exercise of viewing the various combinations could occupy a whole year, so that he could see the inner workings of Heaven in the changing weather patterns, in a human relationship and even in the act of buying and selling, where one man takes up the active role of Shin to sell, and the other buys in the passive and resistant role of Mem, with the money or goods acting as the neutral catalyst, as Aleph. As the Talmud observes, one may perceive the invisible in the visible.

Another use of the letters is to use them to contemplate the paths of the Sefirotic Tree. Here the Kabbalist will perhaps spend an hour each day reviewing the diagram like a mandala to trace the flows of influxes through the various letter paths. He might, for example, see the letters purely as keys to describe the character of a particular circulation between the sefirot, or he might think of them in terms of the words they make up, as certain sets of connections are seen. For instance, the letters Samech, Vav and Gimel, on the paths that bring Hod, Gevurah, Binah and Keter together, spell out the Hebrew root word for 'return to source'. This gives much insight into the pillar of Fear.

Another exercise in the use of the letters on the Tree is for the contemplative to say his Aleph-Bet-Gimel . . . in a continuous chain as he visualizes the Lightning Flash descent of the Tree, with a triad being completed as soon as three sefirot are connected by the prime flow. In this manner he sees, as the Sefer Yezirah puts it, 'the appearance of Ten Sefirot out of Nothing as a Lightning Flash, or glittering flame without Beginning or End. The Word of God is with them as they go forth and return.' To contemplate this unfolding and enfolding flow of letters and sefirot in the mind's eye can lead the contemplative far beyond the first stages of Gadlut and Devekut.

The consideration of the sefirot is the main work of the Contemplative Approach, and their study in relation to one another on the Tree is the first thing an aspirant has to do. This is accomplished by reading, listening, thinking and observing. For example, he may be given Malkhut to study for a month. During this time he reads as much as he can about the heavenly Malkhut, the place of the Shekhinah, and about the earthly Malkhut. This could be in the form of a conventional scientific investigation into matter in its various states, or an examination of an economic system, in which the hardware of goods and services and the accumulation and distribution of wealth reveal the miniature Tree within the sefirah of Malkhut, the Kingdom.

For a more esoteric study, he may plough through many volumes of Kabbalistic commentary and still learn nothing of the Malkhut of Azilut beyond the theoretical knowledge. It is here that the contemplative method comes into its own. It is a curious fact about Kabbalistic work that it is possible to acquire knowledge that under ordinary mundane circumstances is difficult or impossible to find. The method is as follows. A Kabbalist who is under discipline, and so is prepared, can by the act of Kavvanah direct a question deep into his unconscious. This question will be taken up by the level that is appropriate in the upper or inner Worlds, and an answer will be sent down sooner or later, directly into the Yesodic mind of the contemplative, or be presented externally in a situation that he recognizes as the solution to his theoretical or practical problem. This technique has been used for several thousand years by Kabbalists, and has been variously described, most commonly as the presence of a heavenly or unseen maggid. In the case of the aspirant studying Malkhut, such an experience would illuminate his earthly knowledge and perhaps reveal that the Shekhinah was indeed present, even down a coalmine, and that it was possible to perceive It there, if one was in the right spiritual state. Such a realization would be vital to his comprehension that Keter is present in Malkhut, and that the flow of Divine Will and Love reaches even to the depths of Asiyyah.

The study of the sefirot in pairs of opposites is important to the Kabbalist's understanding of how the Tree operates. Therefore the contemplative would at some point devote his time to thinking about the relationship between Hod and Nezah, Gevurah and Hesed and Binah and Hokhmah, because each pair uses the principles of Form and Force or Severity and Mercy in quite a different way. For example, the slow process that goes to make up the understanding of an intellectual concept is quite different from the sudden flash of revelation that presents an idea which could change a lifetime or even history. In order to have some comprehension of the Mind of God, the Kabbalist must study his own intellectual processes, because as an image of his Maker, he has a minute version of the Lord's Intellect. The analogue is clearly set out in the Zohar, in the sections known as the Books of the Concealed Mystery and the Greater and Lesser Assemblies. Here, in the symbolism of the Great Head and in the construction and dynamics of the Sefirotic Tree, the Mind of God is seen manifest, although He Himself remains concealed. To read these books was considered an act of contemplation and many generations of Kabbalists have pondered the pages, if only to trigger off some deep intellectual process within their own psyche.

Another method of contemplation is beautifully set out by the great Kabbalist Moses Cordovero, who like Luria lived at Safed in Palestine in the sixteenth century. Besides his detailed writings on Kabbalistic theory and speculation, he wrote a small book called *Tomar Debhorah*, or the 'Palm Tree of Deborah'. In this the sefirot are contemplated in terms of human conduct, so that a man imitates their qualities in his own life. For example, in his chapter on Hesed he expounds the virtues of loving kindness and how a man should not only love God but his fellow men. He indicates how the sefirah of Mercy should balance Gevurah, to hold the power of the left or Other Side in check. He goes on like this throughout the book, demonstrating in terms of conduct how the Bible and Kabbalistic theory relate the sefirot below on earth to those above in the upper Worlds. Cordovero's preoccupation with checking the power of Evil had a direct bearing on the times he lived in, shortly after the national trauma of the mass expulsion of the ancient Jewish community from Spain in 1492. This event shook the Kabbalists as much as the laymen of the period; there was a great deal of speculation on what had happened in the upper Worlds to effect such a cataclysm, and this produced Isaac Luria's reformulation of how Evil entered the world.

Besides the direct act of contemplation there is its application to prayer. In this technique the Kabbalists have several methods. One is that, as a man says a prayer, he also considers each letter in its Kabbalistic context, so that the whole schema of Manifest Existence is continually being reflected on as he passes from word to word. To do this requires the most extraordinary degree of attention and a real foundation in basic Kabbalistic teaching. Its purpose is not only to perceive the various levels present in the prayer but to break through into a yet higher state of Devekut. To aid this transcendence, prayer-books were especially designed, so that the correct order of sequence in sefirotic progression was used. This caused some problems with the more conventional rabbis, who saw it as a threat to the traditional form of prayer.

Another method is to fix the attention on a particular sefirah while praying. This exercise sets out to invoke that sefirotic principle not only in oneself but in the Worlds above, so that a direct connection is made during the prayer. It is not however without danger, because to invoke a sefirotic archetype in the psyche can lead to an excess of Force or Form. For example, if a man dwells too much on Gevurah, he is likely to become the subject of Judgement, which might be more than he could bear, or become a severe judge in his own right, which would make him perhaps excessively stern in his assessment of others. The reverse is true if he concentrates on Hesed. To be over-merciful at first sight appears to be good, but such a man would be too tolerant and easily allow evil to increase both in himself and others. Then Heaven would have to correct the situation with a dose of Gevurah to clean up a corruption born of neglect. The sefirot are therefore more usually contemplated in pairs, with perhaps an additional emphasis on the weakest sefirah in the aspirant's make-up. Such an exercise would be given by a maggid who would carefully watch over him. The purpose of the prayer itself is to give the operation an emotional power and act as a stable framework for the Kabbalist to hold on to as he engages in contemplation.

In order to enter the Kingdom of Heaven, there has to be a Foundation in Beriah. This means that the abyss that normally separates the non-sefirah of the Yeziratic Daat from Binah and Hokhmah is filled by the paths coming from the Beriatic Hod and Nezah, so that the Yeziratic Daat is transformed into the Beriatic Yesod. In this manner the Beriatic aspect of Outer and Inner Intellect can manifest directly their Understanding and Wisdom in a slowly emerging image based on the Knowledge that has been acquired about the World of Creation. The gradual establishment of a Foundation in Beriah means that a person moves out of the stage of Approach, be it Action, Devotion or Contemplation, into direct contact with this next World. Tradition says that there are veils between the Worlds, and this phenomenon is observed in that we cannot, in the natural state, enter into the World of Spirit, or mystical condition, except by an Act of Grace, or by Avodah, which means work, service and worship. Avodah is the conscious penetration of the Beriatic Veil from below, by Kabbalistic intention and Knowledge.

The Third Garden of the Extended Tree is where the three Upper and three Lower Worlds meet. It is in this middle face of the Five Faces that the human and Divine come into Spiritual communion. Just below this lowest part of Heaven is the Triad of the Soul.

The soul is composed of Hesed and Gevurah, which, according to some Kabbalists, are the Cherubim or angels who guard 'the Way of the Tree of Life', as the Bible puts it. These angels stand before the Gates of Upper Eden or Heaven, on either side of the Way which begins at the Self of the Yeziratic Tiferet. The Way, we have seen, is entered upon only when the aspirant rises out of the vegetable and animal stages of Natural Existence and into the human state of Self-Consciousness, and then of Soul Consciousness. With the conversion of Yeziratic Knowledge into a Beriatic Foundation in the Tree of Creation comes the establishment of a spiritual Yesod, and the birth of an organized body that can enter and perceive a World which hitherto has only been heard about. At this point the expression 'to be born again' or 'anew' takes on a different meaning, for now with a stable Yeziratic or psychological vehicle almost complete, comes the possibility of developing a Spiritual organism by which one may pass safely through the Gates of Eden into the Seven Halls of Heaven.

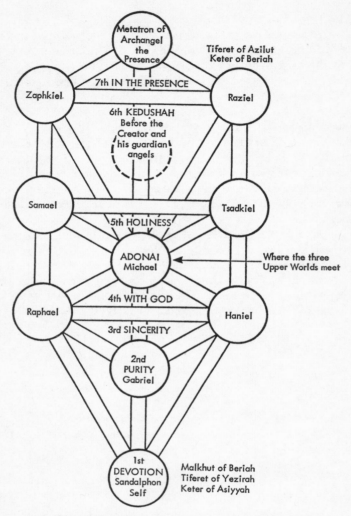

Figure 29. Rabbi Akiba's Ascension. *Here Rabbi Akiba's description of his ascent through the Heavenly Palaces is set out on the Beriatic Tree. Moving through seven distinct states of reality, he passes between the guardian archangels up out of the lower face of Creation into the upper face of Beriah which is simultaneously the lower face of Azilut. Here in Emanation he stood, so he tells us, erect and trembling before the Divine Presence of the Glory.*

30
Ascension

Accounts of ascension into the Seven Heavens of Beriah are to be found throughout Kabbalah's long literature. While they vary in detail, according to the language of the period and the personal imagery of the writer, they have much in common. Thus, it is possible to recognize general parallels in the apocryphal accounts of the ascensions of Abraham, Levi, Moses, Isaiah, Burach, and in the Book of Enoch. The result of such comparisons is a kaleidoscopic impression of realms of experience quite indescribable to natural sensibility; one must be content with a dim and subjective glimpse of the upper Worlds, if one has not received them for oneself. Taking two examples of Merkabah or Chariot Journeys into the Beriatic World of the Throne and beyond, we shall attempt to recapture a faint after-image of a mystical ascent and its steps upon the Extended Tree.

Rabbi Akiba ben Joseph, the great maggid of the first century in Palestine, left a treatise of his journey through the Seven Heavenly Halls or Palaces. In this he describes to Rabbi Ishmael, another master of Merkabah riding, how his inward descent into his own being corresponded to his ascent into the World of Beriah. This account will be matched to the Teaching about the Seven Heavens to be found in the Oral Tradition and in fragments scattered through the Talmud and written Kabbalah.

Before we can follow the ascent into the Upper Worlds, an important metaphysical principle must first be established. According to Tradition there are seven lower and seven higher Halls in the phases of ascent. The Seven Lower Halls may be seen in the seven Yeziratic Sefirot of Construction, which might be considered as seven stages of psychological initiation rising up from the Malkhut of the central nervous system to the Hesed of the Soul triad. There is, however, another way of regarding the Halls, and this is to consider the central triads of consciousness as the progression of states. Thus while the bottommost Lower Palace is still the Yeziratic Malkhut of the bodily Tiferet, the second is the ego of the Yeziratic Yesod or the ordinary mind. This is followed by the third stage in the psychological Tree, that of the Hod-Yesod-Nezah Triad of Willingness, and by the fourth triad (Hod-Tiferet-Nezah) of Awakening Consciousness. The fifth state is the Soul triad of Self-Consciousness, with the sixth (Binah-Tiferet-Hokhmah) and seventh (Binah-Keter-Hokhmah) stages being on the Yeziratic side of the lower face of Beriah. When the conversion of the Yeziratic Daat into the Beriatic Yesod takes place, then the mystic's Self is transformed into the Beriatic Malkhut and he enters the Kingdom of Heaven.

Rabbi Akiba states in his treatise that he entered this First of the Higher Halls of Beriah in a state of devotion. Here in the place of the Self, where the three lower Worlds meet, the Way proper begins. This is where the Vilon or Veil of day and night is rolled back and forth. In the Palace of the Curtain between the natural and supernatural, the Vilon is the frontier where men meet angels. Called the Seat of Faith, this Hall opens out from the physical world of Asiyyah, through the psychological World of Formation and into the Creative Realm of Spirit. This is the hidden door in the Heart of Hearts, through which archangels whisper fragments of knowledge, their coming and going like the brush of a passing wind. Into this, the first of the Heavens, a natural man can enter, sometimes apparently quite by accident, to gaze in awe at the Heavens above, which vanish in the instant he retreats into the Keter of Asiyyah and the safety of his body and sensual reality. At such a moment the drawn veil of Vilon is rolled back over the Self to turn the day of heavenly awakening into the night of spiritual sleep. Only the man of deep devotion and conscious intention can sustain such a vision.

The next stage to which Akiba moved was the condition of Purity. Here the sefirah in the middle of the Third face of the central Garden

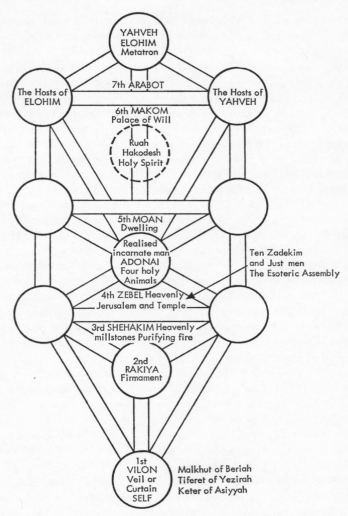

Figure 30. Seven Heavens. *In this scheme the Seven Heavens are placed on the central column, as against the seven lower sefirot in some Kabbalistic formulations. This is because here the Heavens are seen as states of consciousness up the middle Way of Holy Knowledge. As spiritual stages, the traditional accounts set out in symbolism the conditions of each level from the first moment of Self-awareness at Malkhut to the final ecstasy in the Seventh Heaven of Arabot.*

of the Extended Tree is the Second Heaven. As the Yesod of Beriah, it is the place where Gabriel, the archangel, conducts the Kabbalist out of the Daat of Yezirah into the Foundation of Creation. Called in this scheme the lower Rakiya or Firmament, it divides the two upper Worlds from the two lower ones or the natural from the supernatural parts of Universe. It is here that the signs of Heaven are seen. Prophets and the pure in heart may perceive them, but until a man's earthly Daat is transformed into the heavenly Yesod these celestial symbols remain a mystery. It is said, that all the souls who remember God attain this level and enter into the second stage of Devekut or Communion with the Spirit. It is also recorded that this is where the souls of the departed commence their journey upwards into the River of purifying Fire that flows through the Third Heaven above. It is also why Akiba had to obtain the degree of Purity before moving on into the presence of the Archangels of the Beriatic Hod and Nezah, Raphael and Haniel, the Guardians of the Third Heaven.

The Beriatic triad Hod-Yesod-Nezah is the Hall where Rabbi Akiba entered the state of Sincerity. Here in the trinity of the Yeziratic Binah-Daat-Hokhmah is that part of the deep psyche which corresponds to Outer and Inner Intellect and the Knowledge imparted to the Kabbalist who attains this level of Spirit. This is the place of the heavenly millstones which grind the spiritual manna that falls every day to sustain both those whose souls are awake and those who sleep below in the natural world, where the Spirit influences their lives and their being through the unconscious. The word 'manna' is sometimes translated as 'brightness' or 'illumination', and manifests through the sefirot of psychological Wisdom, Understanding and Knowledge. Called the Shehakim or Skies. The Third Heaven is the Palace of Light and Fire, and the place where, it is said, the twenty-two letters of the Hebrew alphabet manifest before entering the Beriatic Yesod, which in the descending Work of Creation becomes the illuminated Knowledge of the Kabbalist engaged in the ascending Work of the Chariot. At such a stage he perceives the relationships between all the sefirot below the Yeziratic Keter: that is, he knows his own psychological nature. This Beriatic triad, which corresponds to that of Willingness in the World below, leads the Kabbalist between the Archangels of Tradition and Revelation into direct contact with the Heart of the World of Pure Spirit.

The Fourth Heavenly Hall, composed of the Beriatic Hod-Tiferet-Nezah, is called Zebul, meaning Habitation. It is said to be the place of the Heavenly Jerusalem. Here Akiba says that he was with God. Being in contact with the Beriatic Tiferet would place him directly under the Azilutic Malkhut, which is occupied by the Shekhinah, the Presence of the Lord. As the Tiferet of Creation, this place is watched over by the Archangel Michael who is guardian to the House of Israel. Immediately below the sefirah of the Shekhinah is the Temple upon whose altar is written the quotation from I Kings 8:13: 'I have surely built thee a House of Habitation, a place for thee to dwell for ever', which indicates the first direct connection with the Eternal World of Azilut. Also to be found here, Tradition says, are the ten great Zadekim who constitute the esoteric or Heavenly Assembly of Israel. They dwell just below the one fully evolved Man who resides in the Yeziratic Keter – which is simultaneously the Beriatic Tiferet and the Azilutic Malkhut – and acts as the incarnate link with the Divine. Oral Tradition states that one such man exists on the earth at any given time, although his presence is openly manifest to the World only when it is needed. To some he is known as the Messiah and to others the Axis of an Age. He has a place and name in every living Tradition. When Rabbi Akiba attained this level of being he came into the presence of the nearest God-Name to natural man: ADONAI – LORD. This is where the human and Divine Worlds meet.

At the fifth stage of his ascent the Rabbi entered the Heavenly Hall called Moan: the Dwelling. Here, before the Archangels Samael, Michael and Zadkiel, the guardians of the Beriatic Gevurah-Tiferet-Hesed triad, he had to demonstrate his Holiness. In this equivalent of the Soul Triad, but in the World of the Spirit, the Archangels of Severity, Truth and Love watch over the intermediary zone of spiritual morality that divides the upper heavenly Garden, which also embodies the lower face of the World of Emanation, from the lower heavenly Garden, that simultaneously contains the higher face of the World of Formation. This intermediary triad is the stage of spiritual integrity, where a Kabbalist attains, on leaving Yezirah, a state of psychological completeness or holiness. In such a condition the Barakhah of God manifests as a divine thunderbolt and reveals, we are told, a vision of the workings of Providence. Such cosmic moments have been described in many ways. Some speak of the Heavenly Supervision of Creation; others of the Four Great Holy Living Creatures, the Bull, the Lion, the Eagle and the Man, who support the Throne of Heaven. Others speak of the dwelling where the purified souls who have reached this level of spirit praise God and are absorbed in the bliss of his Divine

Love. Here, others record, reside the risen or transcendent Patriarchs of Israel and a whole hierarchy of angels and archangels who operate and maintain all the Worlds below the Heavenly Judgement and Mercy of God.

The Sixth Heaven is defined, in this scheme, by the great Beriatic triad Tiferet-Binah-Hokhmah. Here before the Ruah Hakodesh, the Holy Spirit, Rabbi Akiba echoed the Kedushah, the celestial sanctification of the angels. Named by Tradition Makom, which means Place, it is called the Palace of the Will, because here is where the Divine intention is implemented through the Daat of Beriah to bring about Creation. This Daat is also the Yesod of Azilut, and bears the Divine Name EL HAI SHADDAI – the LIVING ALMIGHTY GOD. Thus the Holy Spirit of the Beriatic Daat imparts the Knowledge and Will needed by the Worlds created below. It is also known as the place where 'the Kiss of God' manifests. It is to this level, we are told, that the most conscious of spirits rise in order to integrate with the Will of the Ruah Hakodesh and thus become one with the Spirit. That is why it is sometimes called 'the Place of Death', or where the sense of individuality may cease to be, because the Kabbalist has passed well beyond the fleshly estate. This does not necessarily mean actual physical death, because in this position between the created and the Divine Worlds there is still the choice to go on and yet be able to return.

Rabbi Akiba continued his ascension, so leaving the World of the Chariot below. Fully entering the Tree of the Throne and passing between the two archangels of Binah and Hokhmah, spiritually embodied in the Great Beings of Zaphkiel and Raziel, he entered the Seventh Heaven and stood, he tells us, 'erect, holding his balance with all his might', as his physical, psychological and spiritual bodies trembled in awe of the greatest of created beings, the Archangel Metatron, who as the transfigured Enoch is called the Archangel of the Presence of God in Creation. Here just below the place of the God-Name YAHVE HELOHIM is the Supernal Triad of Beriah, called Arabot of the Seventh Heaven. In this Heaven is the, as yet, undiffused reality of Creation. Here is the margin between potential and actual, as Divinity Wills the Worlds below to be created. This is that place where the Spirit of God hovers over the Deep in the first chapter of Genesis. Sometimes perceived as clouds or a vast plain, two of the meanings of the word Arabot, it is also seen as the vast surface of a cosmic sea. The Hebrew word for 'Heaven' is 'Shamaim', which is composed of the two root words for fire and water. Traditionally the

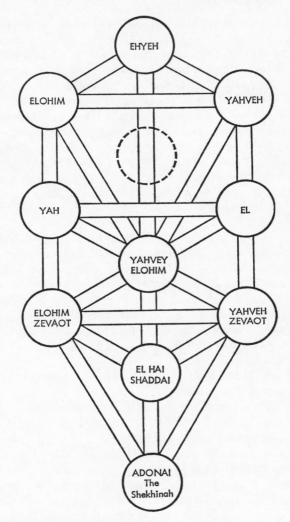

Figure 31. The Holy Names of God.

active pillar of the Great Tree of Azilut is related to fire and the passive to water, with the middle pillar composed of air in the form of the RUAH ELOHIM, the Spirit or Wind of God. All three combine to make the Seventh Heaven, with the element of earth below completing the scheme down through all the Worlds as Force, Form and Consciousness unfold into denser and denser materiality.

Arabot is just below the Keter of Beriah, the Crown of the Creator. It is from this place of the Creator that all created things emerge, descend, ascend and re-emerge. The Act of Creation occurs, we are told, in the utterance of a word. This Word is the first of all sounds to be heard in Manifest Existence. It is the supreme Name of God: EHYEH – I AM. This first of the Divine Names originates from beyond the Keter of Beriah, in the World of Azilut, which is composed of the nine other Names of God and their divine qualities. Known to us variously as the Ten Sefirot, Sapphires, Sparkling Lights, Garments, Vessels and Powers, they are eternally emanated. Should they cease to be, even for an instant, all the Manifest Worlds would vanish. Tradition says that every creature utters the supreme Divine Name on being created and on its return to its Maker. It is the spiritual realization of this Name and its accompanying Divine state that Kabbalists seek while still incarnate, unless they wish to go beyond and so never return from a complete union with the Crown of Crowns.

Kabbalists who have glimpsed beyond Creation into the Eternal World of Emanation speak of One who rides upon the Heaven of Arabot, others of the appearance of a Man seated upon the Throne of Heaven, and yet others of the likeness of Adam to the Glory of God. It is small wonder that Rabbi Akiba stood erect, holding himself in balance as he trembled in awe. When he returned from his ascension, Akiba ben Joseph was, it is said, a man of great knowledge and holiness. And who would not seek these pearls of great price?

Everyone is searching for something. Some pursue security, others pleasure or power. Yet others look for dreams, or they know not what. There are, however, those who know what they seek, but cannot find it in the natural world. For these searchers many clues have been laid by those who have gone before. The traces are everywhere, although only those with eyes to see or ears to hear perceive them. When the significance of these signs is seriously acted upon, Providence opens a door out of the natural into the supernatural to reveal a ladder from the transient to the Eternal. He who dares the ascent enters the Way of Kabbalah.

Editorial Note

The English transliteration of Hebrew differs widely. In this book the *Encyclopedia Judaica's* spelling of Kabbalistic terms is used. However, out of respect for the non-Jewish student of Kabbalah, a table is set out to show the matching spellings used in the Western esoteric Tradition. Also included is a corresponding table of Alphabets.

English transliteration of Hebrew

English translation	Jewish tradition	Western Esoteric Tradition
The Sefirot		
CROWN	KETER	KETHER
WISDOM	HOKHMAH	CHOCKHMAH
UNDERSTANDING	BINAH	BINAH
KNOWLEDGE	DAAT	DAATH
MERCY	HESED	CHESED
JUDGEMENT	GEVURAH	GEBURAH
BEAUTY	TIFERET	TIPHERETH
ETERNITY	NEZAH	NETZACH
REVERBERATION	HOD	HOD
FOUNDATION	YESOD	YESOD
KINGDOM	MALKHUT	MALKUTH

English translation	Jewish tradition	Western Esoteric Tradition
The Alphabet		
A	ALEPH	ALEPH
B	BETH	BETH
G	GIMEL	GIMEL
D	DALETH	DALETH
H	HEH	HE
V	VAV	VAU
Z	ZAYIN	ZAYIN
CH	CHET	CHETH
T	TET	TETH
I	YOD	YOD
K	KAPH	CAPH
L	LAMED	LAMED
M	MEM	MEM
N	NUN	NUN
S	SAMECH	SAMEKH
O	AYIN	AYIN
P	PEH	PE
TZ	TSADE	TZADDI
Q	KOOF	QOPH
R	RESH	RESH
SH	SHIN	SHIN
TH	TOV	TAU

Glossary of Terms

Arabot:	Seventh heaven.
Asiyyah:	World of Making. Elemental and natural world.
Ayin:	The No-Thingness of God.
Azilut:	The World of Emanation: the sefirotic realm and Glory. Adam Kadmon.
Barakhah:	Blessing or Grace.
Beriah:	World of Creation and Pure Spirit. World of Archangels.
Binah:	Sefirah of Understanding. Sometimes called Reason.
Daat:	Sefirah of Knowledge.
Devekut:	Communion.
Din:	Judgement, alternative name for Gevurah.
En Sof:	The Infinite or Endless. A Title of God.
Gadlut:	The major conscious state.
Gevurah:	Cycle of rebirth. Transmigration of souls.
Gilgulim:	Sefirah of Judgement. Literal translation Strength or Might.
Hesed:	Sefirah of Mercy. Sometimes called Gedulah.
Hod:	Sefirah of Reverberation, Resounding Splendour.
Hokhmah:	Sefirah of Wisdom and Revelation.
Katnut:	The lesser conscious state.
Kavvanah:	Prayer with conscious intent: plural Kavvanot or special prayers.
Kellippot:	World of Shells and demons.
Keter:	Sefirah of the Crown.

Malkhut:	Sefirah of the Kingdom.
Merkabah:	The Chariot of Yezirah.
Nefesh:	Animal or vital Soul.
Neshamah:	Human Soul.
Nezah:	Sefirah of Eternity, also called Victory and Endurance.
Pechad:	Fear. Alternative name for Gevurah.
Qlipoth:	Western Tradition spelling of Kellippot.
Ruah:	Spirit.
Sefirah:	Containers, Lights and Attributes of God: plural Sefirot.
Shekhinah:	Indwelling Presence of God in Malkhut.
Shemittah:	Great cosmic cycle.
Teshuvah:	Repentance, redemption and conversion of a lower face into an upper face.
Talmud:	Recorded commentaries on the Bible and Oral Tradition.
Tiferet:	Sefirah of Beauty. Sometimes called Adornment.
Yesod:	Sefirah of Foundation.
Yezirah:	World of Formation. Psychological and angelic World.
Zadek:	A just man.
Zelem:	Image.
Zimzum:	Principle of Divine contraction before Universe comes into being.

Index

73160